THESE WORDS
CHANGED
EVERYTHING

Startling News That Rebuilt a Maya Worldview

David Aeilts
Edited by Roger Peterson

*Our Wonderful friends
Tru & Jean
Who had a part in
in this story
Thank You
Ken & Elaine*

stem PRESS

Minneapolis, MN 55438

THESE WORDS CHANGED EVERYTHING
Startling News That Rebuilt a Maya Worldview

Author: David Aeilts

Editor: Roger Peterson

Publisher and Copyright: © 2009 by STEM*Press*
P.O. Box 386001, Minneapolis, Minnesota 55438-6001, U.S.A.

Cover design, photo insert, Mexico map, and pre-press preparation: Pine Hill Graphics, Eugene, Oregon 97405.

Interior design: STEM*Press*, Minneapolis, Minnesota.

Printing and binding: Bethany Press International, Minneapolis, Minnesota.

Funding for writing, publishing, and printing was provided, in part, by generous gifts from friends of the Chamula Bible Translation project.

ISBN 978-0-9711258-6-5

Printed in the United States of America.

When quoting from Scripture or when referring to Scripture, the Bible, or pronouns used for any aspect of the Trinity, the publisher has intentionally capitalized those nouns (pronouns) as a form of giving honor to God and to His Word. Scripture quotations marked "NIV" have been extracted from the *Holy Bible: New International Version®, NIV®,* copyright © 1973, 1978, 1984 by International Bible Society.

Ordering additional copies: Additional copies of *These Words Changed Everything* can be obtained from your favorite bookstore or by ordering directly from the publisher at: **www.STEMpress.org**

to

DOMINGO HERNÁNDEZ AGUILAR,
who allowed the *Good New Words*
to ignite a spark of faith in his heart,
then dared to tell others

Foreward

"COME IN," I said in response to a knock on the door of my Mexico City office one summer afternoon in 1957. Little did I know that the people walking in that door would play major roles in a drama to be acted out, scene by scene, over the next fifty years. That drama forms the story line of this book.

In walked Ken and Elaine Jacobs, new members of the Summer Institute for Linguistics (SIL), the language development arm of Wycliffe Bible Translators. The Jacobs asked if they could be assigned to translate the NEW TESTAMENT into the Tzotzil-Mayan dialect of the Chamula Indians. I had prayed for a long time that the Lord would send just the right persons to the Chamulas. They had to have a special calling to reach these people with God's Word, and they needed a clear understanding of the difficulties they would encounter.

The fiercely traditional Chamulas represented one of the most challenging assignments in our Mexican Branch. They did not allow outsiders to live among them, and every Chamula within their 1,000 square mile tribal area was rigidly held to preserving their animistic religious and traditional system. Those who dared to question or break tribal norms were either expelled or killed.

As we talked, Ken and Elaine did not waver in their conviction that *The Impossible People* (as some called the Chamula people) was where God wanted them to serve. It was easy to see that they were the answer to my prayers.

Over five decades, and under less-than-ideal conditions, the Jacobs learned the Chamula language and reduced it to written form. Teaching the first Chamulas to read, they initially translated the NEW TESTAMENT and later the OLD TESTAMENT into this indigenous language.

The firestorm that resulted from the translation of Scripture into their heart language changed the lives of the Chamulas, and it changed the translators themselves. Until now, only fragments of this story have been published. But you hold in your hands the whole amazing account—fifty years in the making and told by the individuals who lived it.

What they called the *Good New Words* radically transformed this proud people, destitute and dying, into a vibrant community of faith that has become a success story in the larger Mexican culture. For more than 150,000 Chamula Indians living in southern Mexico today, THESE WORDS CHANGED EVERYTHING.

BENJAMIN F. ELSON
Wycliffe Bible Translators / Summer Institute of Linguistics
Director, Mexico Branch
1957–1965

Acknowledgments

Thanks to:

- *Ken* and *Elaine Jacobs* for entrusting me with a story that sooner or later transforms whomever touches it—I know it has changed me.

- Wooddale Church (Eden Prairie, Minnesota) and Pastor *Tom Correll* for introducing me to the Jacobs by saying, "I know a couple whose story needs to be told."

- *Domingo, Paxcu, Manuel, Tumin, Lorenzo, Chus, Pedro, Maria, Gustavo, Andrés* and *all the Chamula men* and *women* who generously shared with me their individual stories.

- *Al* and *Sue Schreuder* (missionaries of the Reformed Church of America, working with Chamulas under the auspices of the Mexican Presbyterian Church) for translating my interviews with these men and women and for reviewing each chapter to verify its accuracy.

- Author *Hugh Steven* for patiently mentoring me, a business journalist, in writing a non-fiction novel.

- The 30+ people who made telling this story possible by their financial and prayer support.

- My wife, *Nanci*, for her love and encouragement.

DAVID AEILTS
Minneapolis
Spring 2009

Contents

Introduction

ALTHOUGH PENNED in the style of an animated and colorful novel, the stunning story you are about to read is true. Every person you encounter—whether Chamula, Ladino, or American—is real, and each narrative surrounding that person is real. David Aeilts (pronounced *aisles*, like in a church or theater) painstakingly took every reasonable effort to accurately capture the handful of events chosen to represent this much longer, and still ongoing, 50+ year story. When more than one Chamula person shared the same first name (Manuel, for example), we selected a Chamula or Spanish pseudonym to help prevent identity confusion for most of those occurrences.

Who are the Chamula people? How could simple Words sabotage their animistic allegiance to death, poverty, and the 'gift of the gods'? How could such Words cause tens of thousands to forge new lives and permeate their communities with uncompromising hope? You're about to find out ....

ROGER PETERSON
Editor and Publisher
STEM Press, Minneapolis
July 2009

1
Fire On The Roof

THE PEAKED thatched-roofed house seemed cozy enough. Gently bathed in rich moonlight and nestled nearby a large field of placid maize, it spoke of rest and peace. Few could have realized this dreamy, tranquil setting was nothing more than a pretentious backdrop to the treachery marching quietly on stage. Religious elders of the fiercely independent Chamula Indian tribe had issued a barbaric decree: this house—or rather, the people inside—were like rodents. Rodents must be exterminated.

Like so many Indian dwellings in the highland beauty of southern Mexico, the walls of this uncomplicated one-room structure were made from upright poles plastered over with weather-blocking mud. Sturdied by heavy corner posts with beams atop each wall, its no-frills engineering supported the rain-shedding weight of the thick straw roof. Housed inside was an open hearth, a small wooden table, and a few chairs crafted out of white pine, each about the size of children's play furniture. Five reed sleeping mats lay unrolled, bedding their young occupants on the packed earthen floor.

Outside, the docile moonlight danced playfully on a small fence trying to protect the garden plot that delivered cabbages, beans, squash, and natural turnip greens to its tenants. A small enclosure at the side of the house corralled a dozen sheep that provided wool for clothing and manure for fertilizer. Free-roaming chickens, now still and hushed for the night, roosted in nearby trees.

The stage was calm, the setting serene—just like thousands of other households surrounding the tribal center, San Juan Chamula, that sleepy night. In the eyes of the elders however, the people in this house, who now followed a strange God, represented a severe threat to the tribe's religious system and cultural identity. The 'threat' was eighteen-year-old Paxcu *(pahsh • ku)* who was babysitting two nieces and her younger sister and brother—seven-year-old Abelina, her four-year-old sister Angelina, thirteen-year-old Tumina, and ten-year-old Domingo. All were asleep.

In typical Indian fashion, everyone slept nude, using their clothing as blankets. Suddenly Paxcu's dogs began barking, agitated by someone or something going on outside. Still drowsy with sleep, she rose on one arm and peered through a crack in the door. Paxcu glimpsed flashes of orange light. A cold sweat surged through her body as she realized the orange flashes of light were deadly fingers of fire. A quick glance upward served only to confirm her worst fears. Fire was already racing through the thatch; the highly combustible roof would soon crash in and incinerate them all.

The mob of men who came to carry out the elders' decree had lobbed gasoline on the roof, then ignited it. Armed with razor-sharp machetes and muzzle-loading shotguns, they arranged themselves in a semicircle before the only way of escape—the heavy hand-hewn plank door.

"Get up—someone is here to kill us!" screamed Paxcu to the children. She thrust open the weighty door, only to be greeted by Xalic *(shah • leek)*, the vigilante leader, who raised his gun. Xalic fired point blank at the tender young eighteen-year-old.

A blistering blast struck Paxcu in her face and chest. Stunned, she slumped in the doorway, but just for a moment. She knew if she remained where she was, the long wicked machetes would come next. With every fiber in her body engorged by adrenaline, Paxcu sprang from the earthen threshold and ran for the field of maize. Xalic savagely grabbed her, but without clothing Paxcu wriggled free. She bolted out of the inferno, past her stupefied assailants, and into the beckoning, protective arms of the Indian cornfield.

BLAZING fire and heat from the simple building didn't last long. The dogs' barking likewise faded as Paxcu threaded her way through leaves of ripening maize, darting between rows to elude anyone trying to follow. Emerging on the other side of the field, she kept running. Exhausted and thirsty, Paxcu stopped at a small well. But reaching in to scoop the water, her right shoulder and arm refused to respond. Switching to her left hand, she drank quickly and forced herself onward. A short distance farther, Paxcu came to a house and banged on the door with her good arm—but no answer. Pain racked her entire body. Numb with fatigue, she longed to lie down and sleep. Only then did Paxcu realize she was still naked and that blood was streaming down her body. "Here I am," she cried out to God. "I'm going to die!" Fighting the impulse to slip into painless unconsciousness, Paxcu clutched at another thought: "No, I've got to get out of here—I've got to try to reach the house of Matz."

Half walking, half crawling, Paxcu stumbled onto another home first—a kindly neighbor who answered her weakening knock. Aghast at the suffering, pathetic figure collapsing in his doorway, the neighbor quickly roused his family to get up and help. Frightened and shivering violently from cold and shock, Paxcu welcomed some tattered clothing and the neighbor's help getting to Matz's home only a short distance away. A former shaman, Matz had renounced his tribe's traditional gods and placed his faith in a new deity. When he saw the huddled, injured woman before him, Matz prayed to this God who promised to help and give wisdom in time of need. "Lord, what do we do?" he implored.

Still bleeding from wounds now starting to swell, Paxcu moaned and cried, "I'm going to die!"

"Do you know who did this to you?" questioned one of the neighbors.

"I saw only one man," she replied, also telling them of the four children who had been in her care. "I left them behind," she whimpered. "They must now all be dead."

"All we can do is take her to the hospital in Las Casas,"[1] suggested Matz.

---

[1] **Las Casas** — also known as *San Cristóbal*, the full name is *San Cristóbal de Las Casas*. A Spanish colonial city founded in 1528 in the Valley of Jobel, Las Casas is located about six miles from San Juan Chamula, the tribal center.

The neighbors' first idea was to strap exhausted Paxcu to a chair and carry that load on their backs, but Paxcu objected. "That will never work; let me see if I can walk on my own." Strengthened by simple prayer, the small group slowly picked their way across the steep, pine-studded slopes of the Chamula highlands, and down into the dish-shaped Valley of Jobel.[2]

ℰ ℰ ℰ ✿ ? ? ?

IN spite of her nauseating pain, the long winding trek gave Paxcu time to ponder her early life and the events leading up to the horrific calamity just moments ago. Paxcu López Hernández was born in the Chamula *paraje* (village or hamlet) of Sactzu[3] in 1949. Her father, addicted to alcohol used in every religious, social, and political ceremony, died when Paxcu was a child. Her mother taught Paxcu to worship tribal gods of water, wood, and stone. A cross inside the family's home bore resemblance, in shape only, to the Christian symbol imported by Spaniards centuries earlier. Chamulas embraced the *physical* cross as yet another deity to be worshipped and appeased.

Painstakingly selecting her next steps downward, Paxcu started thinking about that cross and the time just after her father died when she was greatly troubled in spirit. She knelt, as she had been taught, to light a candle before that cross. But the candle tipped over, landing in a bed of dried pine needles also used in cross worship. Flames soon ravaged the dry kindling and quickly spread to the entire house. Paxcu's older brother angrily accused her of burning down their home and threatened to throw her into the fire. Despite suffering burns to her own body, Paxcu's mother rushed to her daughter's defense. She could still hear her mother exclaim between sobs, "You are not going to hurt Paxcu!"

Paxcu next recalled how her mother, with a family to support and no husband to help, had followed other Chamulas to work on the low-

---

[2] **Valley of Jobel** — literally *valley of grass*. Before the Spanish pushed them out, Chamula's tribal center was located in this valley.

[3] **Sactzu** — a small village in eastern Chamula territory.

land coffee *fincas* (plantations). Paxcu had accompanied her. But grief struck again. Her mother died at the hands of a Mexican man, only to be improperly buried by non-Chamula *cashlan* (outsiders). Paxcu remembered returning to Sactzu to live with her older sisters Shtumina *(shtoo•mee•na)* and Losha López Ic´alnabil, who by that time had children of their own. Her older brother was away working on the *fincas*. Paxcu assumed the job of caring for the children.

She gingerly took a few more steps, and thought about the day her sister Losha announced, "My son, Mateo, is going to die because of a sickness cast on him by a shaman." Paxcu recalled being taught that shamans served as a bridge between the physical and spiritual worlds, and possessed power to heal or harm. So the sisters had taken Mateo to another shaman who tried his best to counter the harming curse. But the sickness wouldn't break, and the boy still refused to eat.

Next they took little Mateo to Matz, another shaman neighbor. They wanted Matz to conduct a tribal healing ceremony, thinking he'd light candles, drink the local sugar cane liquor *pox* (*pōsh*), and sacrifice a chicken. Paxcu had been taught that a sick person's soul was being eaten by the devil. If a chicken was sacrificed, the devil would often release the human soul and grab the soul of the chicken instead. How surprised they were when Matz refused the sisters' request! "I don't do that any more," he announced. Matz explained that he and a few others in the tribe were beginning to hear about a new deity who not only heals the body but the soul as well.

With her painful decent down the slopes getting more difficult, Paxcu still recalled with clarity what Matz said next. "If you will kneel here, I will pray for you, not as a shaman does, but to the living God. Then there will be hope for the little boy." Holding Mateo in their arms, Paxcu knelt together with her sister while Matz prayed for him. When they returned home, little Mateo Ic´alnabil wanted to eat, and began to get well.

Moved by her son's dramatic improvement, Losha decided to believe in Matz' God. "Why don't you also believe," Losha urged her sisters. "There is a God who heals and takes care of us. He doesn't ask for chickens, money, or candles—He accepts us without any expectations."

Paxcu paused for a brief moment as she savored her reply: "I want to believe." Her older sister and younger brother also professed their trust in this same new deity.

Continuing their step-by-step decent, Paxcu mentally retraced an earlier journey into the Valley of Jobel. Matz, the former shaman, had led Paxcu and her family on the three-hour walk from Sactzu to Las Casas where he promised they would hear more about this God. She remembered gathering with a handful of other Chamulas in a large walled compound owned by Americans, Ken and Elaine Jacobs.

Paxcu reviewed her first impressions of the Jacobs' large yard. She didn't see any temple like she expected, just a few other Chamula people who were worshipping this new God. She vividly recalled hearing God's Word read for the first time in her own language, and without any hesitation, embracing it with her heart.

A Chamula man from the *paraje* Ya'al Vacax, Miguel Cashlan, had taught the small group that day. Though her walk was not getting any easier, Paxcu slowly replayed Miguel's words: "There is a God who loves you and who forgives you. He makes no demands of you and you do not have to pay him." This was a radically different concept for Paxcu and the others, who'd been taught from birth to appease the gods of nature. "There is a God-man, Jesus, who came to earth and offered His life's blood in our place, for the forgiveness of our sins," she recalled Miguel saying. "Your sins are erased. You are free." This, too, was welcome news! "This Jesus suffered and died, was buried, and eventually was raised from the dead," he continued. "And even we, if we put our trust in Him, may well suffer for doing that."

As the small group continued their descent toward Las Casas during the early morning hours following the attack, Paxcu took comfort in those words. In spite of throbbing wounds and painful thoughts of children left behind, she also thought back to Miguel's next statement, which gave her courage to keep going. "If and when it happens that you suffer, be strengthened because the only thing these people can do is kill your body. They cannot take your soul—that is in the hands of God." Miguel had encouraged Paxcu and other young believers not to hide the faith which had given them hope and light. "All of our people are living in spiritual darkness," he said. "Keep telling the good news to every person you meet."

Paxcu had done exactly that. On the trail home from the Jacobs' compound, she told the very first person she met—her aunt, a practicing shaman. Paxcu remembered noticing wounds on her aunt's legs and a bloody rag wrapped around her arm—evidence of ceremonial cutting while under the alcoholic stupor of *pox*. "Why don't you give up your drunken life, and begin to trust in Christ?" Paxcu recalls urging her aunt. Her aunt reacted by spreading the word that Paxcu and other Christians were no longer observing the tribe's religious traditions. Christians began being treated with suspicion and open hostility.

Her pain refusing to subside, Paxcu thought about the many other trips she made to the Jacobs' yard in Las Casas, and how she continued to hear the Scriptures taught in her mother tongue. How thankful she was they weren't speaking the *cashlan's* language of Spanish, which she didn't understand.

After one trip, Paxcu remembered her aunt asking coldly, "Are you still believing in this Christ?"

"Yes I am."

"You better be careful, because you are all going to be killed," revealed her aunt.

"Who in the world would want to kill me?" Paxcu questioned.

Her aunt named a man—the man who later appeared in Paxcu's doorway with a loaded shotgun. "I know Xalic has already bought several containers of gasoline. WATCH YOURSELF!"

Paxcu thought back to Miguel's words: "When your life is in danger, take time to fast and pray and give yourselves into God's care." So on that fateful Friday evening in the autumn of 1967, having fasted and waited on God for three days, Paxcu fed the children in her care from a pot of roasting corn. The five sang GOD PAID FOR OUR SINS WITH A VERY EXPENSIVE PRICE, the only Christian song Paxcu knew at that point. They prayed and lay down to sleep. Then the barking. Then the fire. Then the gun.

❦ ❦ ❦ ❦ ❦ ❦ ❦

PAXCU—wounded and fatigued—arrived in Las Casas about 8:00 A.M. that morning, where they first located Miguel. Paxcu blurted out her story, ending with her conclusion that the children in her house must have been killed. Miguel quickly took Paxcu to the local authorities to report the crime, then right away to the hospital where nurses bathed her, dressed her wounds, and put her on bed rest. Since she spoke no Spanish, Miguel served as Paxcu's interpreter.

The doctor ordered X-rays to determine the extent of her wounds. Results were encouraging. "I can see twenty-one pellets in your head and neck," reported the doctor, "but your heart and your other vital organs are unharmed." Though assured she would not die, Paxcu's suffering lingered those first hours in the hospital. The swelling in her face, neck, and chest increased. Her arms and hands refused to obey her mental commands. Because of excruciating physical pain and the heart-wrenching emotional grief of losing her home and the likely deaths of the four younger children under her care, Paxcu sobbed much of the time.

Miguel returned to the hospital that evening with definitive news on the children. Earlier that day Chamula police found the charred remains of thirteen-year-old Tumina in the burned-out house, and collected them in a pail for later burial. They discovered seven-year-old Abilena, ten-year-old Domingo, and four-year-old Angelina huddled together in a mud bathhouse just yards from the home. Domingo was dead, his head nearly severed from his body by a machete blow. Angelina was alive when police arrived but died en route to the hospital. Only seven-year-old Abelina had survived. A machete slash across her face knocked out some teeth and almost severed one arm, but the bone remained intact. Paxcu and her sister Losha wept uncontrollably.

Miguel tried to console the sisters. He told them the children had gone to be with Jesus and one day they would see each other in heaven. But as new believers, Paxcu and Losha had difficulty grasping this. Then one night three weeks later, Paxcu had a dream. In her dream, Paxcu's sister and brother who were killed in the attack, Tumina and Domingo, appeared at her bedside. Paxcu recounted the story:

"My brother put his hand on one shoulder and my sister put her hand on my other. They said, 'Paxcu don't cry'." In the dream, Paxcu challenged her younger sister, "But you burned up."

"No," replied Tumina, "I haven't burned."

Then turning to her brother, Paxcu said, "You died from a machete."

"No," countered Domingo, "I'm alive in heaven."

Paxcu paused, then asked, "Is our mother there?"

"No," they said sadly. "She's not here. She never heard the Word of God."

Paxcu shared her dream with Losha and told her sister that the children, including Losha's daughter Angelina, had *not* died but were alive and together in heaven. Losha was doubtful, especially since she had seen the children's remains. But the grieving mother had to admit Paxcu's dream confirmed what the new believers were learning as they studied the *Good New Words.*[4] Believers don't die—they go to be with the Lord.

---

[4] The English word for *Gospel* means the *Good News*. Since the early Chamula believers had no actual word for *news*, the English rendition of the Chamula word for Gospel became the *Good New Words*.

2
An 11-Year-Old Savior

NINETY-NINE years before Xalic's tribal posse burned Paxcu's house to the ground, the Chamula people perpetrated another heinous act. But to an animistic people holding tenaciously to their traditional beliefs, it seemed like the right thing to do.

They crucified their own savior.

The Jesus forced on them by their European conquerors—in a language they did not understand—was a *cashlan*. The Jesus portrayed in Spanish art wore a shirt with buttons and shoes with buckles. No Chamula dressed like that. They wanted a savior of their own. Many volunteered for the honor of becoming that savior. Tribal elders chose a young boy whose father and mother were reputable shamans. On Good Friday, 1868, a riotous crowd nailed the eleven-year-old to a cross.

Nineteenth Century historian Vicente Pineda encapsulated this monstrous, substitutive sacrifice with one surreal statement: "[The boy] screamed in pain, in a pitiful and moving voice, which was drowned by the clamor of the devilish mad men, who were drunk on liquor and blood."[5]

[5] **Vincente Pineda** (1888), *Historia de las Sublevaciones Indigenas Habidas en el Estado de Chiapas [History of Indian Uprisings Occurring in the State of Chiapas]*, as cited in: **Bernardo Reyes**, *El Cristo De Tzajal-Hemel [The Christ of Tzajal-Hemel]*. The Reyes publisher, publication date, and page numbers are unknown due to the condition of our manuscript.

Additional background information in this chapter concerning the substitutive crucifixion has been derived from **Diane M. Nelson** (1997), "Crucifixion Stories, the 1868 Caste War of Chiapas, and Negative Conciousness: A Distruptive Subaltern Study," *American Ethnologist, 24*(2), pp. 331–354.

How could mobs of Chamula people nail a child to a cross—or shoot a teenager in the face while lopping off her brother's head? True, rampant chauvinism and the liberal use of *pox* to suppress inhibitions had something to do with it. But understanding Chamula's painful history helps shed more light into this diabolical gloom.

CHAMULAS descended from the ancient Maya people. Even though their earliest settlements predate the Hebrew Savior by 2,500 years, Mayas rose to power in Mesoamerica[6] between 250 to 900 A.D. During their 'Classic' period, the Maya built forty great cities surrounded by intensively farmed lands. These ancient architectural wonders boasted magnificent palaces, public plazas, stone ball courts, celestial observatories, and pyramid-shaped temples—all constructed without aid of metal tools or the wheel. The Maya elite excelled in art, mathematics, and astronomy, developing a highly accurate 365-day solar calendar and a hieroglyphic writing system similar to the one used by the ancient Egyptians.

The Maya worshiped a myriad of deities. Gods most closely related to their agricultural society occupied a prominent place in their belief system—like the maize god *Yum Kaax*; and *Chaak*, the god of thunder and rain. Mayas viewed their rulers as mediators with the gods.

Maya gods possessed both good and bad characteristics and were known for their appetite for human blood. Religious practices centered on appeasing them in many ways, including ritual bloodletting. Priests offered up human sacrifices, and Maya aristocracy practiced self-torture as a means of contacting the gods and preventing wholesale disaster. Moreover, the Maya viewed death as a portal to a dangerous trek through an underworld populated with evil gods.

About 900 A.D., the Maya Empire began to decline. By the time the Sixteenth Century Spanish conquered Mesoamerica, most of these great cities lay in ruin, and Maya civilization had degenerated into a series of small, warring tribal states. Returning to a society based on

---

[6] **Mesoamerica** — a land area occupied by similar cultures and stretching from southern Mexico through Guatemala, Belize, El Salvador, western Honduras, and the Pacific lowlands of Nicaragua and northwestern Costa Rica.

subsistence farming, their descendants forgot most of their ancestors' advances, including reading and writing. Yet they retained many aspects of the Maya's dark, deadly religion.

ᕀ   ᕀ   ᕀ   ☆   ᕂ   ᕂ   ᕂ

THE Chamula people are one of more than two dozen tribes of Tzotzil *(soats • seal)* Indians in the southern Mexican state of Chiapas. A Mayan language group of about 500,000 people, the Tzotzil inhabit a cold, rainy highland plateau at 3,000 to 10,000 feet above sea level. The largest of the Tzotzil tribes is Chamula, with a present-day population of about 150,000.[7]

The European world intersected the Chamula world in the 1520s when the Spanish Conquistadors, aided by warriors from a neighboring tribe, overran a fortress the Chamulas had built to keep out invaders. The Chamulas were forced to relocate their tribal center from the verdant Valley of Jobel where the Conquistadors, in 1528, established a settlement from which to govern the highlands. That settlement, known today as San Cristóbal de Las Casas (or by either of its shortened names, *San Cristóbal* or *Las Casas*), is located about six miles from San Juan Chamula, the tribe's present-day political and ceremonial center.

The Spaniards imported their religion. Roman Catholic priests often accompanied the Spanish military forces with the goal of converting native populations to Christianity. Churches were quickly constructed in tribal centers like San Juan Chamula.

But the same culture that heralded a glorious hereafter also presented the Chamulas with a here-and-now of pain, hardship, and marginalization. Spaniards also carried in their European diseases, to which the Indians had no immunity. Chamulas saw their livelihood erode as Spain granted choice farmland to their victorious soldiers, and later to European settlers. Nor was the hardworking, responsible nature of these Indians lost on the Spaniards who often conscripted the Maya for heavy labor. The Spanish Crown itself 'contributed' 20,000 Indians to

[7] **Alan John Schreuder** (June 2001), *A History of the Rise of the Chamula Church*—Master's Thesis (Pasadena CA: Fuller Theological Seminary, School of World Mission and Institute of Church Growth); and personal email communications between the author and Alan Schreuder during 2008 and 2009.

the Dominican Order of the Catholic Church for the construction of San Cristóbal's first cathedral and convent. Project foremen cut notches in the ears of the workers, many of them Chamulas, as a sign of ownership.

Over the years, the pot simmered. Far from being subjugated and assimilated as perhaps their European overlords hoped, Chamulas retained much of their pre-conquest identity. Social and political customs survived, modified only slightly by the occupiers. Even their pre-Christian religious beliefs survived as they blended adoration of Catholic saints with their own gods of nature.

What the Spaniards (and later the *Ladino*[8] population) had not counted on was the pride of this indigenous culture in their heritage, and their aggressive nature when faced with hardship and loss of tradition. Like the ancient Maya, Chamulas considered life a constant battle between the forces of good that protect human beings and the forces of evil that destroy them. Garnering the favor of the good gods and appeasing or avoiding the displeasure of the bad gods was paramount to maintaining order in the Chamula community. To aid in this process, traditions were established by past tribal leaders, and present leaders were bound to protect these traditions at any cost.

All this pride and zeal for tradition came to a head during the so-called Caste Wars of Chiapas in 1867–1870. During this period of religious and political rebellion, the Chamulas took an unprecedented step to divorce the foreigners' god and legitimize their own animistic traditions. At the Lent season in 1868, the rebellion's leader, Pedro Díaz Cuscat, stood up in the plaza of a Chamula settlement, Tzajal-Hemel, and made this announcement:

> "Now is the time to finish with the people who are not of our blood, whose soul is not the same as ours. They have not the same language or the same customs. We must do this so as not to offend our household gods, who came to stay among us for no other reason than to protect us.
>
> "We don't have to worship an image that represents persons who don't belong to our race, when we have our own images," continued Cuscat. "The images in the churches were made by white peo-

[8] **Ladino** — a Spanish-speaking Central American resident who was not of Indian descent.

ple. In olden times, these people chose one of themselves to be nailed to a cross. They called him the Lord. Every Lent they repeat the crucifixion. It will soon be time for the crucifixion, and I propose that we crucify someone from our town, so we, too, can have a Lord of our own to worship, one who has the same soul and blood."[9]

Passions inflamed, the Chamulas lost what remaining respect they may have had for the Christian religion and ratified Cuscat's proposal. Some suggest they did this as much to protest their bondage under the rule of the Ladinos as to create a new cult. Either way, the native population abandoned the Church's teaching in an emotional show of nationalism. "Chroniclers of the time relate that these peaceful and docile natives turned into fierce men, and the women disputed for the honor of offering their sons for sacrifice that to them meant the complete salvation of their people," observes historian Bernardo Reyes.[10]

The village elders selected Domingo Gómez Checheb of San Juan Chamula, an eleven-year-old son of two shamans, and nailed him to a rough-hewn wooden cross in the town plaza, in place of the Spaniards' Savior with whom they could not identify. The noise of the drunken crowd drowned out the screams of the young victim, according to Reyes. Women collected Domingo's blood and perfumed his body. "Domingo finally died in piercing pain," concludes Reyes, adding, "The cross [they used is now on display ...] in the church of Chamula."[11]

THE Chamulas followed up this act of religious defiance with further religious and political insurrection. They took up arms and killed a Spanish priest and his aids. They attacked isolated Ladino settlements, killing men, women, and children indiscriminately and without mercy— finally laying siege to Las Casas itself. Ladino forces repelled the attack, but not without sustaining a hundred casualties and inflicting forty

---

[9] **Bernardo Reyes**, *El Cristo De Tzajal-Hemel [The Christ of Tzajal-Hemel].* The Reyes publisher, publication date, and page numbers are unknown due to the condition of our manuscript.

[10] *Ibid.*

[11] *Ibid.*

casualties on the Indians. With reinforcements supplied by major cities in the region, the governor of Chiapas counterattacked Chamula's armed men, forcing them to disperse.

The last of the rebels were finally subdued in the remote northern villages in October 1870. Meanwhile, the rebellion's leader, Cuscat, fled to the mountains where he later died.

While the Mexican government succeeded in restoring a degree of political order following the Caste Wars of Chiapas, it failed to subdue the resistant and resilient spirit of the Chamula people. Retreating to their tribal lands, these proud people determined in the years that followed to have as little to do with the outside world as possible. Schooling in Spanish was discouraged among tribal members, except for a select few bilingual scribes appointed to serve as liaisons between the state and the tribal governments. Most Chamulas knew little about the world beyond the highlands. Those who sought temporary employment on coastal coffee *fincas* or ventured into Las Casas to sell to the Ladinos what little they produced, understood only how much the Ladinos despised and marginalized them. The Chamula Indians, in turn, harbored an attitude of disgust toward, and superiority over, the Ladino population.

To prevent cultural contamination, the Chamulas restricted access to tribal areas and refused to permit Ladinos to live among them. Fearing for their own safety, Ladino law enforcement officials turned a blind eye to most reported violations of Mexican law, except for homicide. Only then did they dare venture into the highlands with a well-armed force.

This fierce and most-feared Indian tribe strictly enforced observance of its cultural and religious traditions among its own people. The elders treated any new ideas with extreme suspicion, regarding them as aberrant and dangerous to the well-being of the tribe.

Neighbors and family members were encouraged to report on each other, resulting in an attitude of mistrust that pervaded daily life. Anyone daring to deviate from the prescribed social, political, or religious views of the tribe risked public humiliation and shunning, physical abuse, imprisonment, loss of property, expulsion, and even death.

After the 1868 substitutive crucifixion of Domingo Gómez Checheb, the Chamulas continued to practice a synthesis of animism and Catholicism. They combined Jesus Christ and God the Father with the sun—this became their male god *Ch'ultotic*; and combined the Virgin Mary with the moon and earth to create their female god *Chulmetic*.

Moreover, they assigned attributes to various Spanish saints relating to their animistic traditions. For example, they venerated *San Jeronimo* (St. Jerome) as caretaker of animal souls and patron saint of *j'ilols*, the healing shamans. Chamulas believe each human has a *chanul*—an animal soul companion given to them at birth—in addition to their own soul (*ch'ulel*). Illness or death is interpreted as distress or death of that person's animal or *chanul*. An *j'ilol* must have a particularly powerful animal soul companion in order to intercede with the spirit world in behalf of his/her 'patient.' Many Chamulas are not interested in seeking modern medical attention at clinics or hospitals because western medicine ignores the *chanul*.

By Paxcu's time in the 1960s, control of the church at San Juan Chamula, which tribal members claim still contains the cross on which young Domingo died, had long since transferred from Rome to the Chamula elders. The faithful worshiped ceramic images of saints enclosed in booths lining the interior of the church while shamans practiced their healing crafts inside this same building originally consecrated to the conqueror's faith. Priests rarely visited here, and then only at the pleasure of tribal authorities to administer the sacrament of baptism[12] to newborn infants.

Through the mid-1900s, the Chamulas remained an extremely independent and proud people, expressing no need for anyone's approval. Ladinos and other Maya Indian tribes viewed the Chamulas with trepidation. The prophet Habakkuk, writing about a similar people around 600 B.C., captured it perfectly: "They are a feared and dreaded people; they are a law unto themselves...".[13]

While their traditional isolated lifestyle was in many ways comfort-

---

[12] Chamulas believed baptism attached the soul to the body.

[13] HABAKKUK 1:7/NIV.

ing and insulating from all that the corrupt outside world could throw against them, it was also dark and sinister. Most Chamulas were constantly looking over their shoulders at who might want to do them harm. The burdensome costs of their *cargo* system—which required males to perform a year of political and religious service at their own expense—kept Chamulas in perpetual poverty, as did their tradition of subdividing farmland between sons and daughters. The entire cultural system was designed to punish anyone who aspired to rise above the rest or to provide progressive leadership.

Moreover, their cultural system failed to provide an adequate mechanism for dealing with change that was happening at a rapidly increasing pace.

Most disheartening were their spiritual traditions which offered little hope beyond their difficult, fleeting lives. Stretched between their ancient Maya heritage and an increasingly global world, Chamulas may have continued to exist in isolation and spiritual uncertainty had not the Living God spoken powerfully to the hearts of a few tribal members willing to risk all they had for the priceless gift of Life.

But first, a way had to be found to speak His Word to the Chamula heart.

❮ ❮ ❮ ✿ ❯ ❯ ❯

PROVIDENCE intervened in the form of an American Christian named Cameron Townsend. Townsend's Summer Institute of Linguistics (SIL) contracted with the Mexican Department of Education in 1935 to develop writing systems for 150 tribal dialects spoken by the indigenous people groups within its borders. Mexico considered its seven million Indian citizens as its greatest wasted resource. They neither produced what Mexico consumed nor consumed what Mexico produced. Developing a system of writing these languages would advance the government's objective of communicating with these people groups, a necessary stage to include them in the greater community.

The purpose of SIL (a sister organization of Wycliffe Bible Translators) was to bring spiritual, intellectual, and emotional light and freedom to indigenous communities—communities enslaved for centuries by their dark animistic traditions. Under the terms of their agreement with the government, SIL would teach each people group to read and would translate literature of high moral character—including the NEW TESTAMENT. Townsend reasoned that those who read such translations of Scripture would actually hear God speaking in the language of their hearts.

In the late 1950s SIL assigned Ken and Elaine Jacobs the task of developing a written form of the dialect spoken by the fiercely independent Chamula Indians. The Jacobs wondered how they could accomplish this task with such a foreboding people. Since Chamulas hated outsiders, living among them to learn their language was out of the question. As a first step to this nearly insurmountable task, the Jacobs established their initial home in the old Spanish colonial city where Chamulas came to trade, San Cristóbal de Las Casas. Ken and Elaine thought if they could live in Las Casas where the Chamula people did their 'outside' trading and business, that somehow they might establish a connection with this aggressive tribe. So aggressive and isolated were the Chamulas, that some locals labeled them *The Impossible People*.

3
Unpacking The Chamula Soul

SEVEN YEARS before Paxcu fled bloodied and naked from her burning home, two mismatched men sat outside together, oblivious to the late afternoon sun as it edged nearer the peaks surrounding San Cristóbal de Las Casas. The shadows grew long against the adobe brick walls as Ken Jacobs labored with his language helper, Juan Pérez Jolote.[14] They worked together at a hand-crafted wooden table daubed in yellow paint. Dressed in his stately black woolen *chamarro*,[15] the sixty-year-old Maya Indian, a civil and religious leader in his tribe, listened intently. He responded patiently as this *cashlan* half his age attempted conversation in the older man's dialect—*Chamula Tzotzil*. Ken hoped to master, and eventually devise, a system of writing the Chamula language. But first he must discover its basic elements including the alphabet, proper punctuation, what constitutes a clause or sentence or paragraph, and how to restate metaphors and similes to avoid distortion of their meanings. Ken's curiosity must have seemed endless as he probed for the language's rules and nuances.

"Who do the Chamulas pray to for rain?" asked the young linguist, searching for a new topic. Ken recalled that ancient deities like *Chaak*, god of rain and thunder, had new identities in the post-classical Maya world.

Energized by the new topic, the old man's face brightened, and his shoulders rose to their full stature against the straight-back chair. Ignoring

---

[14] **Juan Pérez Jolote** — Juan is *John* in English or *Xun* in Chamula. Jolote means *turkey*. Historically, Chamula shamans sacrificed turkeys during healing ceremonies. Later, chickens were substituted as more economical.

[15] **Chamarro** — sleeveless woolen tunic, knee-length and fastened at the waist with a leather belt. A black Chamarro is sign of authority.

the young man's query, he replied with a question of his own. "Canuto," asked Juan, using Ken's Spanish name, "Have I told you how the gods gave me a prayer for rain?" Ken put down his pen. Many times during the past two years, Juan had interrupted their language sessions to speak of his importance in the Chamula religious and governmental system. It was these 'interruptions' that gave Ken important insights into the lives and culture of the Chamula people who were fiercely protective of their traditions.

As linguists with SIL, Ken and Elaine were under contract with the Mexican government to develop a system for writing this unwritten Mayan dialect. It was Ken's goal to teach the Chamulas to read and write their own language, and eventually to translate God's Word. To accomplish both goals, Ken had to first learn the Chamulas' language and cultural traditions which impacted the structure and usage of that language.

Thoughtfully, Ken picked up his pen and once again held it at the ready. Ken was all ears. Now satisfied he had Ken's undivided attention, Juan described at length how a deity had appeared to him in a dream and given him an invocation to be recited in the fields and at the waterholes of Chamula when the clouds withheld their bounty.

"Of course," said Juan to Ken matter-of-factly, "I did not immediately go out and tell everyone my dream. First, I must understand if this new prayer was, in fact, from the gods." Introducing a new prayer or anything new to this fiercely traditional tribe was never to be undertaken lightly or without considerable thought and planning. More than one well-meaning Chamula in Juan's memory had found himself banished, beaten, or killed for suggesting a change in the tribe's religious, economic, or social traditions—all of which were intricately intertwined. As a tribal leader, Juan himself had given consent to kill other deviants seeking to subvert the tribe's time-honored way of life.

How could this ambitious yet tradition-bound Chamula man reveal a new prayer for rain without being branded a renegade? Juan decided on an age-old approach to this task. He purchased several bottles of *pox*—the alcoholic beverage considered to be the 'gift of the gods.' Chamulas used *pox* as a holy drink in all religious ceremonies. This holy drink was also used in civil ceremonies, and to herald an important conversation between individual Chamulas—like the conversations Juan was planning to have.

Next, Juan donned his finest *chamarro* and slung a *nuti*[16] containing a bottle of *pox* over his shoulder. One by one, and quite inconspicuously, he approached the homes of tribal elders, beginning with the *presidente*, the man responsible in a given year for overseeing all of Chamula's community and religious activities. The *presidente* was commonly referred to as 'the man with the mouth,' and his favor was crucial.

At the threshold to the president's house, Juan called out the customary greeting: *Mi li ´ oyote, muc tot?*. . . "Are you there, older father?" (Chamulas rarely used their actual names in greeting one another or in taking their leave, for fear a *brujo*[17] might speak their names before the gods in a curse.)

From inside the darkened doorway came the response: *Li ´oyune, ochan tal*. . . . "Here I am, come in."

Ducking inside, Juan pulled the bottle from his *nuti* and offered the sugar cane liquor to his host. Together they drank. "Why are you here?" his host finally asked. Juan stalled for a time, insisting the visit was nothing special; but both men knew better.

Cautiously, Juan probed his host's mind and attitudes—talking casually about dreams and the importance of dreams in the Chamula culture. Finally, after more conversation and drink, Juan determined the time was right. He thoughtfully and respectfully related the words of the prayer that had come to his attention in a dream. Then he waited for what must have seemed like an eternity. Mercifully, instead of a suspicious glare, the elder closed his eyes and nodded reassuringly. "I once had a similar dream."

Juan left the president's home that evening feeling both relieved and elevated by this first significant confirmation of his encounter with the deities. In successive evenings, he visited each of the elders' homes with *pox* and received similar words of affirmation. He had passed the tests of the spirit world and its representatives on earth—the traditionalists.

"That is how I learned the gods had most certainly given me this

---

[16] **Nuti** — an Indian tote bag slung from the shoulder.
[17] **Brujo** — a harming shaman.

prayer," said Juan proudly. "To this day, if you stand at a waterhole anywhere in the highlands of Chamula, you will hear the *j'ilols* reciting my prayer for rain."

ᛞ ᛞ ᛞ ☙ ᛞ ᛞ ᛞ

Anyone watching Juan and Ken conversing in the waning sunlight that late afternoon in 1960 would have remarked, "They make a strange pair." On one side of the yellow wooden table sat an aged Indian dressed in traditional garb, determined to *insulate* Chamulas from contamination by the outside world. On the other side sat a young American missionary linguist working under the full authority and blessing of the Mexican government, determined to *help* Chamulas interact with the outside world. Unlikely companions, yes, but each man had something the other desperately needed.

Juan possessed excellent command of both Spanish and Chamula—a rarity in his tribe that had not yet mixed to any great extent with the nearby Ladino culture. A bilingual language helper of Juan's caliber was exactly what Ken needed to acquire an understanding of the Chamula's unique Indian dialect.[18]

Confident in their own superiority as respective people groups, each of the various southern Mexican Indian tribes looked down on the other tribes which could not speak their dialect. This was especially true of the Chamulas. They were known for taking aggressive, sometimes violent, measures to separate themselves and to prevent their tribe's cultural integrity from being influenced by other tribes or by the majority Ladino population. Yet here was a Chamula traditionalist, Juan Pérez Jolote, working as a language helper for a *cashlan* in a major Ladino city.

To the aging Chamula leader, Ken offered a nearby source of income. When needing cash, most Indians would leave home for months at a time to work in the *fincas*. But Juan had to walk a relatively easy six miles from the doorstep of his home *paraje* in Cuchulumtic

---

[18] In the Mexican state of Chiapas, Mayan dialects divide into five language groups: Tzotzil, Tzeltal, Tojolobal, Ch'ol, and Lacandon. Chamula is one of at least two dozen dialects and sub-dialects within the Tzotzil language group. In order for Ken to learn the Chamula dialect, the translator (Ken) and the indigenous language helper (Juan) had to share a common language to work efficiently and effectively. They used Spanish, since Spanish was the language of commerce and a bridge language in SIL's translation efforts in southern Mexico.

to reach the Jacobs' home in Las Casas. More importantly, Ken Jacobs represented to Juan an opportunity for reconnection with the outside world he had experienced early in life, coupled with a ready source of respect and admiration he failed to achieve in that world. Juan, now a very traditional Chamula, had once lived as a *cashlan*. Juan had learned the words and customs of the Ladinos because he had spent his early years among them.

℘ ℘ ℘ ✖ ? ? ?

AS he sat with Ken that unseasonably warm early spring afternoon, Juan allowed his mind to wander back to his beginnings. He thought of how he'd run away from home as a boy, because his father beat him repeatedly. He remembered how he'd worked for families in neighboring Indian tribes and how one of them had sold him to a Ladino for two sacks of corn. Finally, the Mexican authorities had discovered the runaway and returned him to his family. But the beatings continued, and Juan ran away again. He worked his way from one coffee *finca* to another, eluding his father who came looking for him, by moving frequently and changing his name.

Instead of his father, more serious trouble found Juan. He witnessed a murder and was jailed when he refused, either through fear or loyalty, to testify against the killer. Although he understood a few Spanish words prior to his incarceration, it was in jail where Juan learned to speak the language well. Juan recalled how, after a year of imprisonment, the government conscripted him and his fellow prisoners into the military to fight rebel armies. While a soldier, he learned to write Spanish, was wounded once, was captured once, and fought for three opposing armies. Then he was released.

Failing to find a place in the Ladino world, Juan felt the irresistible pull of home. He made the long journey back to Chamula. When he finally stood at the door of his family's dwelling, now several years older and dressed in Ladino clothes, he was barely recognizable to his family. Juan looked and even sounded like a Ladino, having lost command of the Chamula language after several years away from his tribe. "I felt like one who was reborn as I learned the language again at my mother's knee, the way I did when I was a child," he said to Ken.

The longer Juan stayed with his natural family—who now welcomed him without question, re-tutoring him in the Chamula culture—the more he felt at home. After the uncertainty of the Ladino world, he was strangely comforted by the rigidity of the tribal traditions linking religious, economic, political, and social activities like an umbilical cord supplying life (or death) to every Chamula.

Juan recalled how he had thrown himself, with unrelenting abandon, into the business of living the traditional Chamula life. This included:

- Worshiping the Chamula gods of the caves, woods, and water, as well as the images of saints introduced by the Spaniards;
- Choosing a wife from a neighboring family and receiving his share of the family land to grow corn like his father and grandfather;
- Constantly advancing his standing in the community by agreeing to serve in various civil and religious offices.

Above all, having witnessed indescribable turmoil and uncertainty outside the tribe, Juan dedicated himself wholeheartedly to the idea that things would not change in the traditional Chamula world—not if he could help it.

If he had doubts about the traditional system to which he had returned, he kept them to himself. True, the myriads of gods the Chamulas served demanded much and offered little. Their representatives on earth were the *j´ilols* and the *brujos*. These shamans kept the average Chamula perpetually poor by requiring the purchase of *pox*, herbs, candles, and chickens used in healing and cursing rituals. Then there was the matter of marriage, which brought with it the subdivision of highly eroded land, parceled out to both sons and daughters. This meant every succeeding generation was also handed a greater dependence on working *outside* of Chamula territory in order to make a living and provide for their families. Finally, there was the tradition of public service—the great equalizer. The Chamulas who did succeed in getting ahead financially were often conscripted to fill civil and religious offices at their own expense. Those with ambition to rise to the top of the system often had to lower themselves to the depths of debt and drunkenness to do so.

Juan could testify of that. Fascinated by the honor heaped upon tribal officials, he and his new wife Dominga made a pact to do 'whatever it takes' to rise to the top of their tribal hierarchy. Over the years, Juan spent thousands of pesos and consumed hundreds of bottles of *pox* to advance from office to office within the Chamula religious and political system, until reaching his current position of honor and responsibility. Was it worth the price he paid? Juan doggedly clung to the hope that it was. After all, he reasoned, hadn't a Ladino author thought him important enough to write a book about his life?[19]

That book, *Juan Pérez Jolote: Biografía de un Tzotzil*,[20] rested securely on Juan's lap as he sat on a bench in front of the *cabildo* (town hall) in San Juan Chamula one afternoon. It was during Q´uin Carnival[21] in 1958. A festival such as this was one of the few times when Chamulas admitted outsiders into their political and religious center. During the festivities, a slender Anglo named Ken Jacobs approached the great man. In his not-quite-polished Chamula, Ken told Juan he'd read his book. Flattered that someone had taken personal interest in his life and impressed with this North American's attempt at his tribal language, Juan agreed to tutor Ken in the Chamula language.

As he worked with Juan, Ken marveled at this lavish resource teeming with understanding about what it was like to be Chamula. Ken wrote to his friends back home in the United States: "If you have ever sat down with an interesting book and slowly and thoughtfully turned its pages, you have some idea of what we are experiencing with this sixty-year-old Chamula. He is a brilliant man. He speaks slowly and clearly and seems to open his soul as he discloses some of Chamula's secrets. Strange and weird indeed are the tales and woes of this people."

---

[19] Background information for this paragraph and other portions of this chapter have been derived from: **Ricardo Pozas** (1962), *Juan: The Chamula: An Ethnological Recreation of the Life of a Mexican Indian*—English Edition (Los Angeles CA: University of California Press).

[20] **Ricardo Pozas** (1952), *Juan Perez Jolote: Biografía de un Tzotzil*—Spanish Edition (Mexico: Fondo de Cultura Economica).

[21] **Q´uin Carnival** — a three- to four-day festival celebrated just prior to Lent.

Ken even constructed a small building for Juan to live in during the work week. The building doubled as a garage on weekends when the esteemed man made his way back into the highlands to be with his wife and to perform the duties of his office. Juan recently had been named to the high office of *Presidente Fiscal*[22] of the Catholic Church at San Juan Chamula.

But Juan's responsibilities as church official extended beyond the confines of the Chamula highlands. "People would come to our home in Las Casas, while Juan and I worked together, to get his opinion," said Ken. Once, Chamula officials brought an Indian woman accused of adultery, in order to be judged by Juan.

Juan pulled a special string out of his pocket and drew it around the woman's head. As he explained to Ken, "If the ends of the string touch, the girl is guilty; if not, she is innocent—but I have the ultimate authority to decide her guilt or innocence."

For two years, Juan conversed with Ken in his native tongue and eventually helped translate a book of thirty-five animal stories—the first written form of the Chamula language ever published. "I could never tell him what we were preparing to do," reminisced Ken, with a tinge of regret. "If his fellow traditionalists knew we were studying the language in preparation for translating the NEW TESTAMENT, Juan's life would have been in grave danger."

THE majestic hills surrounding San Cristóbal had all but swallowed the sun on that temperate spring evening. Juan finished telling the story of his fame and the favor of the gods in choosing only him to deliver a prayer for rain to the Chamula people. In the twilight, Juan paused and looked down at his beautiful black *chamarro*. Something caught his eye.

At his advanced age, Juan wondered occasionally about his choice to embrace the tribe's traditions and where that decision had led him. Now was one of those times. Despite the fame and status he'd achieved, Juan still needed to work outside the tribe to pay for his basic

[22] **Presidente Fiscal** — religious and ceremonial leader of the church.

needs. His health was declining. His hands shook with alcoholic tremors. Like his father before him, he had not been able to satiate his appetite for liquor after many years of ceremonial drinking.

He looked closer at the richly woven cloth of his black outer garment which announced his position as an important tribal official. Then he remembered. A month earlier he had pawned this beautiful cloak (painstakingly woven by his wife) for a bottle of *pox*. The Ladino liquor dealer carelessly threw the garment on a pile of grain sacks. When Juan returned to redeem it several days later, the rats living among those sacks had eaten big holes in his costly black *chamarro*.

Suddenly, Juan realized the scornful contradiction between the highly esteemed Chamula he had just described himself to be, and the pathetic reality of his own empty life. Still looking down, he began to sob, his tears falling on the smooth yellow tabletop. Slowly, he looked up at Ken and with trembling fingers pointed to the gaping holes in his garment. "Canuto," Juan whispered softly, all boasting gone. *Q'uel avil ti c'u j'elan....* "Look and you will see what I am really like."

A short time later, in 1961, Ken and Elaine returned to the United States for their scheduled twelve-month furlough. While they were gone, Juan Pérez Jolote died. Later, Ken wrote these words in a letter to his supporters:

"Juan came to live with us in San Cristóbal for two years until his alcoholic death. He helped us take those first baby steps in learning to speak the Chamula language. In many ways, he showed us the soul of the Chamula people. Although he never helped translate a single verse of Scripture, he was the first of many Chamulas God used in bringing about the most important change their world would ever experience."

In the span of just two years, both men forged an unlikely kinship which allowed Juan to unpack the deep mysteries of his soul. The Jacobs moved a step closer to translating and writing Juan's language. The Chamulas moved a step closer to the *Good New Words.*

4
The Blood Talks

PASCUAL WAS DYING. His skin was pale and felt like wax. His swollen stomach looked hideous and repulsive. Lying on his cot, he writhed in searing pain. Trying to help ease the man's misery and discomfort, a Ladino ranch worker had given Pascual an aspirin. News of the aspirin therapy led residents of Mitzitón, a small 'breakaway' Chamula community, to speculate about the cause of the illness. "Pascual has swallowed a poisonous pill that will not come out," they whispered.

Several local *j'ilols* (healing shamans) had been consulted. None could remedy Pascual's deteriorating condition. Heeding the indigenous folk methods for curing an illness, each of these traditional healers set about to diagnose the cause of the evil holding Pascual's body in its deadly grip. Rejecting the outside world's notions of infection or contagion, their diagnosis began with these questions:

"Have you fallen down or been frightened recently?"

"What have you done against the gods?"

"Whom have you offended?" and "Have you denied favors or services to relatives or friends?"

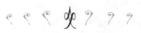

CHAMULAS believe there is a limited amount of supernatural power available in the world. Such power abides within humans, animals, trees—essentially in everything. According to tribal tradition, if you are successful in obtaining more goods than others, you became a success at someone else's 'power' expense.[23] Therefore, nobody in this animistic culture tries to be superior to his neighbors by accumulating a greater number of goods. They fear offending their neighbors, and they fear the *brujo* (harming shaman) will, for a fee, invoke spirits capable of striking down the individual judged responsible for the misfortune of another.

Consequently, one of the first things a healing shaman does is to probe who might want to harm his patient. To determine the cause of the illness and whether it was caused by an enemy, the shaman takes the patient's pulse. The *j´ilol* starts by checking the wrist and inside elbow of the patient's right arm. The healer then performs the same diagnostic procedure on the patient's left arm. Chamula pulse-takers believe 'the blood talks' and can provide messages which they alone can understand and interpret. Through this divinely given gift of revelation, the shaman can determine the identity of the enemy and of his counterpart who cast the curse. In such a case, the shaman may recommend the death of the person who caused the illness.[24]

Chamulas believe sickness can also come from disrespecting tribal boundaries and traditions that rule the community's everyday life. An upgraded tile or tin roof (when everyone else in the village has a thatched roof) would be seen as a display of personal wealth. A physical malady like Pascual's is often considered divine punishment for such an infraction. Loss of a person's *ch´ulel* (soul) through a fall or scare, or the death of a person's *chanul* (the soul of a companion animal born at the same time), may also produce illness and eventually result in physical death.

ᕍ ᕍ ᕍ ✄ ᕃ ᕃ ᕃ

WHATEVER his transgression or misfortune, Pascual's problem perplexed the most sagacious of healers in Mitzitón. With confident finality they said, "There is nothing more that can be done."

In desperation Pascual summoned yet another shaman. At the

---

[23] For this reason, Chamulas carefully save their nail clippings or locks of hair. Should another person find them, that person could extract power from them.

[24] Historically these diagnoses accounted for a high number of homicides within the tribe.

same time, Pascual's wife Maruch summoned the couple's *cashlan* neighbors, Ken and Elaine Jacobs.[25] "Do you have any medicine for him?" she pleaded. "He is so sick." When Ken offered to take Pascual to a doctor in Las Casas, the shaman insisted on going with them.

"This event became our indoctrination to the tragedy of animism," said Ken. On the ride to Dr. Ovideo's clinic in Las Casas, the shaman sat in the back seat of Ken's red Dodge and mixed gun powder with water. He served the liquid concoction to Pascual in a gourd.

After his examination, Dr. Ovideo dismissed the idea that Pascual's distended abdomen and wrenching pain were caused by a poisonous pill. "He has a kidney stone blocking the urinary tract, and that blockage has become infected," declared the doctor, who considered Pascual's condition extremely serious. "He must enter the hospital immediately and have the stone surgically removed."

Pascual and his shaman huddled in the corner, deep in conversation. By this time, Ken understood enough of the Chamula language to know they lacked confidence in the Ladino doctor's diagnosis and feared the treatment. In Chamula experience, no one goes to the hospital until they are extremely sick. When they do go, it is usually too late for effective treatment and they often die. As a result, most Chamulas view the hospital as a place of death rather than a place of health and healing.

Finally the shaman announced, "We must return home immediately to apply our own remedies to Pascual's sickness." Pascual and the shaman begged Ken to drive them back to Mitzitón as soon as possible.

Dr. Ovideo was dumbfounded. "You must convince him to stay!" the physician pleaded with Ken. "If this man is not hospitalized, he will surely die."

For Ken, it was an odious decision. If he could somehow compel Pascual to remain, the Ladino doctor might be able to save his physical life—but if Ken forced the issue, he would surely lose credibility with the Chamulas. On the other hand, failing to intervene would virtually guarantee that Pascual would suffer an agonizing death.

To the doctor's dismay, Ken aligned himself with Pascual, refusing

---

[25] In addition to their residence in Las Casas, the Jacobs maintained a residence in Mitzitón from 1957 to 1964 in order to live as closely and safely as possible to Chamula language speakers.

to force the dying man to remain in Las Casas against his will. "We are living with these people and must abide by their decision. In any case, he will not stay," he informed Dr. Ovideo. Ken helped the hurting man back into the Dodge and began the nine-mile drive back to Mitzitón.

OVER the course of the next two days, the shaman subjected Pascual to many treatments ranging from swallowing worms to sacrificing chickens. At one point, Ken watched in horror as the shaman kneaded his patient's swollen stomach like a giant mound of bread dough, while the stricken man bellowed in pain.

Without modern medicine, Ken realized the only way he could show real concern for his neighbor was to stay with Pascual during the ordeal of traditional treatment. Most of it was horrifying to watch. "In some instances, where his practices bordered on humanity, I assisted the shaman," admitted Ken. He added, "The medical doctor had given me some pain killers which I offered and administered to the patient only at the invitation of the shaman."

Within forty-eight hours Pascual died. A small stream of blood dribbled from the corner of his mouth. When the body was prepared for burial, Ken observed Chamula tradition. He stood with the men of the tribe, facing the corpse of his neighbor, and wept.

"It was our first decision to allow a man to die by his own choice, and it was an absolutely unnecessary death," claimed Ken. He later wrote of the shamans' treatments: "I believe their intentions were only to cure the man; however, their methods were based on centuries of pagan darkness."

In the days and weeks that followed, no one offered an explanation for Pascual's death while in the care of the traditional healers.[26] It wasn't until a couple years later Ken began to understand how Chamulas could reconcile their high esteem for the shamans' wisdom in treating disease with the frequent lack of positive results. The answer

---

[26] In the same way modern medicine glorifies the specialist, the Maya traditional system elevates shamans with greater mystical powers. When a shaman fails at healing, Chamulas often talk about a famous shaman in a distant *paraje* who could have saved the patient. "If only he could have gotten there and had enough money to afford the cure," is a common lament.

came from Ken's friend and language helper, Juan Pérez Jolote.

After hearing the story of Pascual's death, Juan said, "Every man has his counterpart [*chanul*] in an animal. Pascual's counterpart was a coyote. At the same time that young man had fallen ill," explained Juan, "someone had shot a coyote and killed it. Consequently, there was nothing that could save him." In effect, Pascual had died when the coyote died. Ken mentioned to Juan how blood flowed from his neighbor's mouth when he died, and Juan replied confidently, "That's the reason!"

CONVINCED their decision not to interfere in Pascual's treatment was the right one, the Jacobs' compassion only deepened for the Chamulas, whose language and culture they were still trying to understand. In the years that followed, this compassion eventually expressed itself in a medical ministry that saved the lives of many Chamulas who, like Pascual, had exhausted the resources of traditional healing. More importantly, it introduced them to the Great Healer of both body and spirit.

"We are winning friends and gaining confidence among the Chamulas, but the roots of their dark culture grow very deep," wrote Ken, shortly after Pascual's death. "Oh how important that they hear the claims of Christ on their hearts. How necessary that He change their darkness so there will not be this unnecessary waste of human life and soul."

At their Mitzitón residence the Jacobs kept a small supply of drugs like penicillin for infection, erythromycin for tuberculosis, terramycin for eye infections, and other medicines effective against parasites and malaria. At first they distributed these medications sparingly to their Chamula neighbors, lest they be regarded as attempting to harm them rather than restoring them to health.

"It's a science—one cannot just guess," wrote Elaine of the shamans' craft and the Chamulas' view of appropriate treatment. "We are discovering that the coldness or the hotness of the sickness determines if they require cold or hot medicines. Along with the medicine, the shaman must tell the patient what foods they can eat—either cold or hot! A hen chicken, for instance, is hot, while a rooster is cold. Black beans are hot, while others are not."

Sitting with men of the tribe following Pascual's death, Ken heard the shamans blaming the 'cold' pill the Ladino ranch worker had given Pascual, rather than the 'hot' remedy it was claimed to be. Ken would later write, "We are waiting on the Lord to show us medicines and relationships with other Chamulas that will be received as helpful. We certainly don't want to make a serious cultural mistake that could jeopardize our ability to work with these people."

Yet, with the sadness of Pascual's death, there were bright spots. One of these was a twelve-year-old girl, Luz, suffering from uncontrollable dysentery, whose mother Elaine Jacobs had befriended. For more than a week the young girl lay in a gloomy corner of her family's smoky hut. Her dehydrating body, tormented by fever, was slowly withering away. Her drunken stepfather kept himself in a constant stupor, while Luz's mother tenderly kept watch. Faithfully she trusted in the shamans' treatments, ever optimistic as each traditional cure proved unsuccessful. Elaine longed for the mother to ask for help before her daughter's frail body was too weak to respond to medicines Elaine could provide. After nine days, the fearful mother finally accepted her *cashlan* friend's assistance—and the dying daughter slowly returned to life.

Then there was Carmen, from a *paraje* two or three miles away. Reaching down a rabbit hole, the wiry hunter had been bitten by a snake. He stood outside the Jacobs' house early one morning, weak and infirm—peering through the cracks in their bedroom wall to see if the couple was awake. Ken quickly dressed and came to the door. Carmen had wrapped a jungle vine tightly around the top of his right arm. On the end of that arm, his swollen hand resembled an inflated rubber glove.

Q'uel avil ta xicham! . . . "Look and see—I'm dying!" he bellowed out to Ken.

5
You Say I Am Free

I T WAS SHAPED like a stovepipe, courtesy of the jungle tourni-
quet. The entire length of Carmen's arm was filled with angry welts
where shamans had punctured his skin with cactus needles, a routine
treatment for snake bite. Carmen's bloodshot eyes and contorted
expression told Ken the man was in pretty bad shape.

The Jacobs rushed Carmen to a Las Casas hospital run by the
Mexican Institute for Indian Affairs (INI). There a doctor put Carmen on
bed rest and administered anti-venom injections. Ken paid the bill,
informing his new acquaintance, "If you live, Carmen, you owe me
eighty pesos."

Several days later, a much healthier Carmen sat happily on the
Jacobs' porch. His right hand was carefully bandaged and a package of
penicillin capsules stuck out of his pocket. Carmen chatted contently
with fellow Chamulas as he sharpened his saw, getting ready to cut lum-
ber. *Oy cabtel. Oy quil. . . .* "I have to do some work. I've got a debt."

Little by little, the Jacobs successfully treated sick or wounded people like Carmen and Luz, earning their neighbors' confidence. Once
when the tribe experienced a health epidemic, Elaine approached the
INI Medical Center for medicines and an INI doctor offered to come
out to Mitzitón. The Jacobs announced to the community that a doctor
would be available to treat them at their home. On the appointed day,
about twenty Chamula Indians came through the couple's door to see

the medical doctor.[27] Although the doctor spoke fairly good Chamula, most of the Indians would turn to Elaine and ask, "Is the medicine he is giving us any good?" This indicated to the Jacobs that some of the Chamulas in Mitzitón were beginning to have confidence in Ken and Elaine for their physical well-being.

"We trust that, in time, they might see the Lord Jesus in us and learn to trust him for their souls as well," wrote Elaine to friends in the United States.

Not everyone in Mitzitón understood the Jacobs' motives. Some viewed their offer of medical assistance through the lens of a shaman, whose mission it was to both heal and to harm. One Chamula man spent almost half a day at the Jacobs' busy home, engaged in conversation with Ken. Finally, when no one else was around, the man asked Ken if he had any medicines. Ken indicated he did and asked the nature of the sickness, so he could dispense the appropriate drug.

"The sickness tearing at his heart was a terrible hatred," reported Ken. It seems a lady friend of his wife was living in their house. The man found this woman unbearable and was plotting her murder. He wanted Ken to give him medicine that would kill her. Ken refused and the man left. Several days later he showed up again, still thinking Ken would aid him in the crime, just like any other shaman would do.

DOZENS of Chamulas found help at the Jacobs' home in Mitzitón, but Elaine yearned to do more. Although she had some training in treating tropical diseases, Elaine often had to guess at the illness plaguing anyone coming for help. Many times she could only treat the symptoms and not the actual cause. Some, especially babies, died despite her best efforts.

The Jacobs took their first extended visit back to the United States in 1960, where Elaine took a course in parasitology. This helped her learn how to better diagnose many of the Chamula illnesses she was seeing. A family in Minneapolis provided Elaine with a high quality microscope.

---

[27] Many more stayed away, however, for fear of violating tradition or of submitting themselves to a medical system they did not understand.

"With this equipment and schooling, I was able to return to Mitzitón, and look for the real reasons for their illnesses," commented Elaine.

Parasite infestations resulting from poor personal hygiene, inadequate food preparation methods, and contaminated water accounted for much of the sickness plaguing the Chamulas. By using her microscope to analyze stool samples, Elaine could now identify the specific parasite causing the sickness. Her simple but effective laboratory enabled Elaine to prescribe the correct treatment and save many more babies and adults—after the shamans' traditional methods had failed.

The Jacobs' medical efforts among the Chamulas received another significant boost that same year when the couple acquired a large walled property within San Cristóbal de Las Casas. This new two and a half acre property served as their primary residence and translation headquarters for nearly two decades. It also served as Elaine's medical clinic.

Because they feared reprisal and distrusted the *cashlan*, many Chamulas refused medical treatment offered to them by the Mexican government. Over the years, government clinics built and staffed within tribal territories remained largely unused; Chamulas preferred the traditional treatments offered by their own shamans.

In spite of their deep-seated distrust of all outsiders, thousands of Chamulas and other Maya Indians poured into San Cristóbal de Las Casas daily to sell the agricultural products they grew—maize, beans, potatoes, and squashes—along with their carefully-crafted handmade goods like harps, guitars, tables, chairs, baskets, and grinding stones. This daily flood of Indians pouring into the ancient colonial city included the sick and dying who had been treated (unsuccessfully) by the shamans and were told, "There is no hope for you."

These desperate, but daring, Indians—many of them parents with ailing children—slipped silently behind the safety and seclusion of the high walls surrounding the Jacobs' large new property. Here they could anonymously seek help from 'The Woman with the Magic Machine.' "At the beginning, it was the microscope and medicine that brought the people in," said Elaine, whose renown was growing.

Sometimes she allowed patients to peer into the microscope and see the hookworm in larval form, wriggling on the slide. Amazed, they would shout excitedly, "She's found it! She found what is killing little Lucas!"

When Elaine identified the cause of the illness, she would administer the appropriate drug[28] to the patient, often caring for her patient for days. Eventually the Jacobs built a lean-to clinic against one wall of their roomy property, with beds to accommodate Elaine's patients and their families. Travelers needing a bed would also check in here on occasion.

If an illness proved difficult to diagnose or its severity was beyond her ability to treat, Elaine would take the patient to a local doctor. She maintained cordial relationships with several doctors and clinics in Las Casas who didn't particularly like working with the Indians, but admired someone who did. In these cases, Elaine served as interpreter between the patient and doctor, who routinely accepted Elaine's initial observations and lab analysis without question.

The trickle of Chamula people initially visiting the Jacobs' new compound in the early 1960s soon became a flood. Lines formed early in the morning and stretched down the street as they waited for the clinic to open. In 1964 the Jacobs gave up their rented house in Mitzitón because the Chamulas were readily coming to them in Las Casas.

Even those whom Elaine could not help (their condition was either beyond Elaine's abilities, or they had arrived too late for her treatment to be successful) still benefited from her compassionate care. Elaine introduced them to a new concept, that of a benefactor or a 'Savior' who would not only heal their physical diseases but free them from the diseases of the soul.

❧ ❧ ❧ ❧ ❧ ❧ ❧

THE woman and her man slowly, painstakingly approached the Jacobs' high-walled compound in Las Casas late one afternoon. At age twenty-eight, her husband, gaunt and stooped, had already dwindled to less than eighty pounds. His wife, a relatively small woman, now towered over him. The pair had spent their meager resources—plus other money borrowed at a high rate of interest—on several shamans, hoping to find a cure for the man's persistent, progressive illness. As a last resort, they

---

[28] In Mexico, medicines like penicillin, quinine, and drugs to fight parasite infestations could be purchased without a doctor's prescription.

traveled barefoot from their home *paraje* in a remote, mountainous region. He had to lean on her during most of their nine-mile journey.

The couple had heard something about a female *cashlan* in Las Casas with a machine that could work miracles for patients on whom the shamans had given up. It was risky to seek help outside the tribe, especially for these two who lived in the spiritually dark community of Tsonta Vits—the self-proclaimed witchcraft center of Chamula. Still, increasing numbers of tribal members admitted finding physical relief from their suffering, thanks to Elaine, the new non-traditional healer.

As they approached the entrance to the Jacobs' courtyard, the man and woman clung to each other, speaking in low tones. "Will she consent to see us when she learns we can afford to pay nothing for her healing arts?" they worried, then resolved, "We must try. She is our final hope." They rapped softly on the wrought iron gate.[29]

A slender figure appeared. Even at her unpretentious 5′ 2″ when wearing shoes, Elaine Jacobs towered over them. Her skin was white and her hair was dark—not vigorously black like theirs. Her eyes were light brown. Theirs were dark brown. To their amazement, this *cashlan* did not even ask who they were or why they had come. She simply opened the gate and welcomed them in their own language.

Their hostess introduced herself as 'Elena,' the Spanish equivalent for Elaine. She led the couple across the yard and into the front room of her home. This living space doubled as an examination area, with the legendary microscope occupying a prominent position on the table in the middle of the room.

"We've come for medicine," blurted the Chamula woman, offering no names.[30] Her eyes downcast in embarrassment, she proceeded to explain their situation. No money. Last hope. "Can you help us?" came her feeble plea.

Instead of rejection, the couple received comfort from this foreign lady's gracious manner. They secretly wondered how Elena (Elaine) was able to speak their Chamula language.

---

[29] In many developing nations, knocking or rapping on a gate is the equivalent to knocking on a door or ringing a doorbell.

[30] Many Chamula people do not give out their real names, fearing their names will be uttered in a shaman's curse against them. Instead, they talk about themselves and each other in the context of a place or event, such as "the one who fell down by the waterhole."

During her initial conversation, Elaine gently probed for clues to the unseen source of the man's sickness. His physical appearance was already speaking volumes: sunken eyes, anemic complexion, abdominal distension, lesions and blisters on his lower legs and feet. A stool analysis soon confirmed a severe infestation of hookworm and other parasites. Realizing the complex nature of his medical condition, Elaine asked her husband Ken to transport them all to a local clinic. The clinic's doctor confirmed Elaine's diagnosis and prescribed drugs to combat the parasites. Since hookworm attaches itself to the intestinal walls and insidiously saps the body of blood, the doctor also provided Elaine with the medical items needed for an intravenous blood transfusion.

"I've never done that before," she protested.

The doctor replied matter-of-factly, "Well, you're going to learn now."

Medicines in hand, the Jacobs returned with their guests to their home with the big walled yard. It was now late in the day. Elaine prepared beds for the couple inside the Jacobs' little clinic. She began that very evening to administer the prescribed treatment.

They remained with the Jacobs for many days. The Chamula woman watched and marveled at Elena's tender care. Unfortunately the stricken man's condition worsened. His treatment had started too late to reverse the many months of parasite damage. One gray morning the man gave up his struggle, and drew his last breath. His troubled wife trudged slowly toward the Jacobs' residence. "He's gone," she told Elena. The Chamula woman hesitated and then murmured almost imperceptivity, "Will you help me?" Though seemingly dispassionate, her physical demeanor and plea for even more help betrayed the widow's desperate situation. If her husband had died at home in Tsonta Vits, she would have begun wailing, and neighbors would have known there was a death. Her neighbors would have helped wash and wrap his body, and dug his grave for burial—a necessary portal for the entrance of the man's soul to the underworld. As it stood now, the poor woman and her dead husband's body were virtual prisoners in the brick-walled yard of a foreign healer. This violated tribal traditions and placed the well-being of his soul at risk. Her trouble was beyond description.

"Yes, of course I will help you," replied Elena in the Chamula language. Working together, the two women laid boards across the top of a wheelbarrow and used this makeshift gurney to transport the man's body to a water faucet in the courtyard. There they propped him in a small chair, washed him, then dressed him. It was late afternoon by the time they finished. It was then that the Chamula woman revealed her desperate plan.

"I'm going downtown to find someone with a horse," she confided in Elena, hoping to find a kinsman who'd agree to drape her husband's body over his animal, cover it with cloth, and quietly transport it back home to Tsonta Vits. But when she arrived, the marketplace was deserted. Around sunset, she returned to the Jacobs' yard. Fear had tightened its grip on her heart. "There was nobody there for me," she whimpered. As twilight shadows reorganized themselves into the darkness of night, her situation grew more desperate, more hopeless.

In her grief, the new widow allowed her thoughts to wander to the Festival of the Dead. Her tribe observed this ritual every year at the end of October. During this rite, each Chamula family invites the souls of departed relatives back from the underworld for a visit. Families make elaborate preparations, including special foods, clearing weeds from family graves, and marking the way to the houses where the deceased were born and lived their natural lives. "How will my husband be able to find our house, if he is not buried in Chamula?" she wondered, sobbing softly.

Lost and alone in her painful thoughts, she didn't notice Elena approaching her husband Ken and speaking to him in their foreigners' language.

"Ken," said Elaine in English, "We must help that lady."

Ken looked up from his language work. "How in the world can we help her?" he asked, his voice tinged with skepticism.

"She must get his body back into the tribe," insisted Elaine. Elaine paused for a moment, then urged, "Let's take the body up the mountain in our car."

A narrow, stony government road wound part of the way into the mountains toward Tsonta Vits; the rest of the journey would have to be completed on foot. Earlier Elaine had spoken with Lol, an Indian man living temporarily in the Jacobs' large yard. Lol offered to help the woman carry her husband's body from the point where the road ended. Still, Ken doubted their chances of success. He understood that outsiders were not welcome in the highlands, especially after dark. A few years earlier, tribe members hurled stones at their car in broad daylight, despite having a respected tribal elder, Juan Pérez Jolote, with them. The journey Elaine proposed tonight would be much more risky. Sensing his wife's unwavering commitment to the newly widowed Chamula woman, Ken consented.

The widow watched with a small glimmer of hope as Canuto (Ken) retrieved an old canvass tarpaulin used to cover a trailer. It was dirty and stained with oil, but it would have to do. With Lol's assistance, he wrapped the body in the tarp and placed it in the trunk of the Jacobs' 1958 Chevy. Delaying their departure for safety reasons until after midnight, Ken drove his wife, the Chamula widow, Lol, and the dead man's body—stuffed in the trunk—up the meandering mountain road.

No one said a word on that pilgrimage. Each person understood the danger. They had all conspired to transport a corpse, and hide it from both the civic authorities and the zealous Chamula traditionalists. How would they respond if tribal police stopped them and asked what they were doing? Fortunately they never found out. By about 3:00 A.M. that morning the schemers reached the end of the narrow, stony road. They stopped and opened the trunk. Rigor mortis had set in. As they struggled to extract the rigid body, Ken thought to himself, "I might actually have to break the dead man's legs in order to get him out." Mercifully, they freed the corpse without having to resort to this tactic, then positioned it on Lol's back.

The moon emerged from under the clouds. It cast stark shadows on the rugged footpath as the widow and Lol, flinching understandably under the dead weight, began the cumbersome assent to Tsonta Vits. At the first turn, they looked back to see the Jacobs still watching, but soon Lol and the woman had scrambled out of sight. They continued upward, unchallenged through the first *paraje*, then the second, then the third. Except for the annoying barking of the villages' ever-vigilant dogs, the dead man's final trek home was pleasantly uneventful.

❦ ❦ ❦ ❦ ❧ ❧ ❧

SEVERAL days later, someone knocked on the Jacobs' gate. Ken opened the gate, surprised to see the wife of the dead man they'd helped smuggle into Chamula territory. Slung over her shoulder was a bulging *nuti*, obviously containing something very large. Hardly acknowledging Ken, she asked briskly, "Where is the woman?" Ken pointed to where his wife was. The widow brushed by him, walked up to Elaine, and opened her bag. Inside was the old canvass tarpaulin used to transport her husband's body. She had scrubbed it clean—by hand—until it was dazzlingly white.

Soon after her husband's traditional burial, this still-grieving widow had borrowed a little soap. She'd gone down to a nearby stream and spent hours scouring the old canvass that had faithfully carried her lost breadwinner back to his ancestral home. Squatting at the edge of the riverbank, she had pounded the fabric against a flat rock to dislodge years of dirt and oils. There was little doubt she wept while laboring—partly from her loss, but also in appreciation for a *cashlan's* kindness. This kindness took her heart by surprise.

The widow handed the spotless canvass to an astonished Elaine and uttered a simple, but shocking, phrase: *Col a val....* "Thank you." Then she turned on her bare heels, retraced her steps out the gate, and disappeared into the street.

What was so remarkable about her 'Thank you' was that this phrase is rarely ever spoken by Chamulas. *Col a val* literally means, "You are saying I am free—liberated—no responsibility!" The expression is spoken by a beneficiary to his or her benefactor as a means of recognizing a free gift.

In the Chamula culture, under the tribe's animistic belief system, no one ever gives or receives anything free of charge. If an Indian does something for someone else, he requires payment in kind. In the unlikely situation where a no-charge transaction does take place, there is no acknowledgement. As a result there are no benefactors or beneficiaries.

Outsiders are oftentimes surprised by this. Previously, when the Jacobs gave medicine or provided a ride for a Chamula person, the Indian would just take it without a word, then move on. There was no expression of gratitude. The *cashlan* doctor who treated Carmen was offended that his snake bite patient simply walked out the hospital door when feeling better. "He didn't even say thank you," the doctor had protested to Ken.

The Jacobs were learning more about the Chamulas' animistic belief system. Things like the apparent lack of gratefulness (and lack of benefactors or beneficiaries) began to make sense to Ken and Elaine. So did the fact that Chamulas hid any extra goods they might accumulate—because they did not want to be perceived as being greater or more successful than their neighbors. A central piece of the Chamula worldview is based on balance, and the shamans (both the healing and harming shamans) exist to make sure no one gets ahead of anyone else. It helps explain why many Chamulas are reluctant to wear their best clothing in public. It helps explain their non-committal answer when asked the question *Mi lec oyot?*... "How are you today?" They never respond with, "Thanks, I'm wonderful today. Feeling good!" How could they attain that level of success without doing it at someone else's expense? It also helps explain why a good Chamula will seldom accept a free gift from another, because that would mean indebtedness to that benefactor. *Equal to* or *level with* everyone else is the correct place to be in the Chamulas' animistic worldview.

The Chamula widow, overflowing with gratitude toward Elaine, uttered a phrase completely out of character. By speaking the words 'Thank you!' she was saying, in effect, "I am the beneficiary of your kindness," and "I see you as my benefactor." She was accepting the fact that one whom she considered greater had granted her mercy and grace in time of great need.

Not until Christianity began to take hold of the Chamulas' hearts did Chamulas begin acknowledging benefactors and beneficiaries. It was in Elaine's free and unexpected gift of her talents, her time, and her compassion that the widow caught a glimpse of Jesus Christ. In years to come, this woman and hundreds of other Chamulas would finally be able to hear the Savior's welcome words: "You are spiritually free—liberated from your sins—no responsibility to pay Me back for the gift of eternal life that I have given you."[31]

---

[31] The widow later did become a believer (a follower of Jesus Christ).

6
Cracking The Code

ONE OF THE most daunting obstacles Ken and Elaine Jacobs faced was the difficulty of cracking the Chamula grammatical code. Residents of the breakaway Chamula community at Mitzitón taught the couple their first words and phrases. It wasn't easy, however. When Ken and Elaine began to get discouraged by their inability to unlock *all* the rules this complex verbal language required, God provided a human key.

ONE late fall morning in 1957, shortly after sunrise, José painstaking-ly worked his way from row to row in the family cornfield. Although the soil was badly eroded from years of cultivation, it still produced a mea-ger harvest of the golden grain—a staple in the Chamula diet. Weeks earlier José had followed the same path, bending stalks over to hasten the drying process. Now he plucked the small ears and placed them carefully in a burlap sack which, when filled, he'd store in a corner of his one-room house. Growing at least part of the corn his family con-sumed each year kept José in touch with the land and in harmony with the traditions of his ancestors. The remainder of the corn needed he purchased with wages earned as a day laborer, unloading trucks for Ladino shopkeepers in San Cristóbal de Las Casas.

From the market town of Las Casas to his home at Mitzitón was about nine miles. José walked that stretch of highway both ways, at least twice a week. The young Chamula knew only this local segment of the 30,000 mile Pan American Highway stretching from Fairbanks, Alaska, to the lower regions of South America. Out of Las Casas the Pan Am Highway exited to the south, leveling off at about 6,500 feet above sea level. Over the next eight miles, it climbed another 1,000 feet into southern Mexico's beautiful tall pine tree forests. Just before the road began its long, graceful descent to the Guatemalan border, a collection of huts with peaked, thatched roofs appeared on either side of the road. This was Mitzitón.

José put down his burlap sack, filled just halfway with his harvest. He patiently surveyed the smoke oozing from the chimneyless thatched roofs, melding into a fog-like haze atop the simple homes. The vapor blanket drifted slowly over patchy corn fields planted on the hillside, resting at the feet of stoic pine trees keeping watch nearby. On the grassy knoll above, a Chamula woman tended sheep, her coarse, hand-woven black wool *serape* (shawl) wrapped tightly to ward off the early morning chill. On the road below, another woman bent under her load of dry sticks. The fuel would soon stoke her cooking fire and chase back the numbing fall weather now seeping through cracks in her stick-and-mud hut.

This was the way it had been for many harvest seasons prior, with one exception. Three outsiders had moved to Mitzitón and now lived among José and his people. A Ladino landowner—upon whose land the Chamula residents of Mitzitón surreptitiously built their huts—had rented out the ranch foreman's house to Ken and Elaine, known to locals by their Spanish names Canuto and Elena. Together with their daughter Joyita,[32] these newly arrived *cashlans* set out to meet their Chamula neighbors and to begin learning their language.

At first the local residents hesitated to associate with the fair-skinned newcomers. After all, the elders governing the affairs of Chamulas living in the tribal highlands on the other side of San Cristóbal had long prohibited outsiders from living among them. They feared contamination of their way of life and tampering with their ancestors' traditions.

On the other hand, San Juan Chamula, their tribal center of government, was far, far away. Since José and the others in Mitzitón lived *outside* of tribal lands, they could afford to be a bit more tolerant of the outside world—after all, they were 'outsiders' themselves.

---

[32] **Joyita** — Spanish for *Joyce,* meaning *jewel.*

The first resident to have close contact with Canuto and Elena was José's *compadre*[33] Pascual,[34] whose home was close to the ranch foreman's house. Recognizing the newcomers would be ill-prepared for the raw temperatures at these elevations, Pascual had sent his daughter, Josefa, to the Jacobs' door with a bundle of firewood.

That one simple act removed an invisible barrier in the community. Other residents gradually, curiously made their own contact with Mitzitón's newest residents. At first, that contact was limited to glances, the occasional smile, and just a word or two. Canuto and Elena spoke little Chamula and the townspeople spoke little Spanish. But José and others could tell the fair-skinned family was determined to learn their language. Many obliged by naming objects as the Jacobs pointed to them. "*Ants*" (woman) they in-toned as Canuto pointed to a woman. The corn the *ants* ground into dough was *ixim* and the stone on which she ground the corn was *ton*. Deftly, the woman shaped the dough into *vaj* (tortillas) to bake over her wood-fueled fire.

As they walked the dirt paths linking doorways throughout this small, rural community, the curious foreigners always carried pencils and paper. Willing responses to the Jacobs' frequent inquiries resulted in a good deal of marking on that paper. Ken realized that each new word they learned brought them one step closer to translating God's Word for the Chamula people. But the foot traffic wasn't just one direction. Some bolder, more inquisitive Chamulas ventured to the ranch foreman's house now occupied by the Jacobs. They'd spend hours on the porch watching Canuto hand craft wooden toys for the young children in Mitzitón. When their shamans' efforts failed, a few even visited the Jacobs' home to seek relief from the variety of medicines Elena stocked for that very purpose.

As the Jacobs entertained their guests or ventured into the community, they learned increasingly more words and phrases. This enabled them to enter into deeper conversations with their neighbors. Hardly anyone refused to repeat what they'd just spoken, so that Canuto and Elena could get it written down.[35]

---

[33] **Compadre** or **Comadre** —a close friend who has become a baptismal god-parent to a couple's child.

[34] **Pascual** — *cf.* Chapter 4.

[35] "Sometimes our language helpers are so drunk that it's difficult to know just what they are saying," said Ken in

José and his neighbors watched as the Jacobs formed their rudimentary understanding of the tribe's language. Although he did not comprehend their motives, José respected the couple's attempt to meet his people on their own terms—unlike most outsiders who demanded Chamulas learn Spanish in order to communicate.

The outsider approached José the following spring, as the Chamula man worked to clear and plant his cornfield. Ken had offered to give him a helping hand. This is Ken's account of the day, recorded in a May 1958 letter to his North American friends:

"Recently, the Indians have been raking the corn stalks into piles with three-pronged sticks they cut out of the woods. Later, these piles of stalks are burned before the new crop is planted. I asked one of the Indian men named José to cut me one of those sticks. I said I'd help him in the field. He gave me a quizzical look, like he wondered why I would want to do that, but the following day he handed me my stick.

"As I worked along one end of his field, the raking process took me close to another Chamula hut. I wasn't necessarily enjoying this primitive way of doing things, but suddenly I appreciated what I was hearing. A group of ragged native children, dressed in their burlap-type clothes, were calling my name. As I lifted my head to look at them, they would drop their gaze—sometimes turning their backs and laughing. Over and over they repeated their self-made game. I enjoyed it along with them, as I pretended to work.

"This was the first time one shy little girl had ever spoken a single word to me. It was so simple. Suddenly, I realized that she, nor the other kiddies, were afraid anymore. At some point since we had moved among them, perhaps as they sat around the fires at night with their parents, they had heard good words about us. Previous fears they had entertained, either inhibited or suggested, were disappearing. There, in that eroded, smoky cornfield, I thanked God for these friendships. He has answered your

[continued from previous page] correspondence dated 1958, referring to the Chamulas' liberal use of alcohol in daily life. "At times like this, we need our handkerchiefs to wipe off the spray as they put their faces close to ours so we can hear all of the strange sounds, but the language is coming."

prayers that we may make real progress in the language and that
the friendly reception we have received may continue."

José watched with interest as the Jacobs continued to build friendships
and learn the Chamula language. Early many mornings, children of the community, no longer afraid, would gather at the Jacobs' door. They wanted to
see the outsiders up close, and talk with them. These were primarily girls,
since most boys were already working with their fathers in the cornfields.

Whenever they assembled, Elena would bring out a book of pictures
clipped from magazines. As the children identified each image in the picture book, she wrote down the word and its pronunciation, further
expanding their vocabulary. This ritual continued until one day when
several mothers came to the Jacobs' house and complained, "We don't
want our girls to come here anymore. They're supposed to be watching
the sheep, but they want to come to your house," they explained.

Undaunted, the Jacobs found other ways to interact with their
Chamula neighbors. They bought cookies and hard candy, needles,
thread, and ribbon in bulk at San Cristóbal that they sold to their new
friends in Mitzitón.[36] As their presence in the community became more
and more accepted, Canuto and Elena were invited into their neighbors'
homes as well. "They're still outsiders," thought José one day as he sat
across from the Jacobs who, like him, had been invited to a wedding
reception for a young Mitzitón couple. "But they are no longer strangers."

LEARNING words was one thing. But understanding the rules governing a complex language like Chamula was another. The Jacobs needed
to learn these rules to accurately translate Scripture. This proved a
much more formidable challenge than the couple had anticipated. For
a time, the Jacobs maintained residences in both Las Casas and
Mitzitón. During that time, they employed several language helpers,
including Juan Pérez Jolote.[37] These helpers assisted the linguists in

---

[36] Selling needed items to one another is a culturally acceptable way to encourage visits to a person's home.

[37] cf. Chapter 3.

expanding their vocabulary, developing an alphabet, and publishing a children's picture book of animals. Little by little, the Jacobs advanced in their understanding of the *Chamula Tzotzil* dialect.

After Juan's death in 1961, Ken struggled to find a language helper who was both willing and capable enough to assist him. One day in the spring of 1962, a young Chamula man—Domingo Hernández Aguilar— rapped sharply with a small, pointed stone on the heavy wrought iron gate at the Jacobs' home in Las Casas.

"I was looking for work as a gardener," recalled Domingo. "A relative who came to Elena for medicine remembered the many fruit trees in the Jacobs' yard."

Ken refused his services at first. "We have no need for a gardener," he replied kindly. As the linguist turned away, Domingo looked past him to the courtyard and its tangle of undisciplined fruit trees.

Leaving the Jacobs' gate, Domingo made his way down the cobblestone streets of the old city, continuing his search for work. An hour later, a car pulled alongside him. It was the Jacobs. Peering out the window, Ken asked almost apologetically, "Would you come to work for us? We really *do* need a gardener."[38]

That admission proved to be an understatement. In the first few weeks, Domingo transplanted the many fruit trees into straight rows, checking them diagonally to make sure they were spaced with equal distances. He pruned away the dead branches, and when the trees began to set fruit, he braced the weakest limbs to prevent breakage under the weight of their bountiful produce.

As the rainy season approached, Domingo planted beets and carrots in the Jacobs' garden, caring for it as if it were his own. While he worked, Domingo would visit with Ken in his native Chamula language. The young man had superb diction. Ken could hear the grammatical accents clearly, identifying the inflections and intonations which differentiated various words.

As exacting as the young man was in speaking his heart language, he was equally insistent that Ken get the language right. No occurrence illus-

---

[38] Elaine overheard Ken's conversation with Domingo and pointed out the young Chamula man's potential as a language helper—including his ability to speak Spanish. The Jacobs jumped into their car and searched the streets of Las Casas until they found him.

trates this better than the time Domingo's wife Verónica came for a visit.[39]

"I was thinning the beets in their garden," Domingo recalled sheepishly. "Instead of removing the smaller ones, I would pull some of the nicest, healthiest beets and hand them to Verónica to take home and eat."

"At some point in my work, Canuto observed my mischief and tried to reprimand me in Chamula," continued the beet thief, now smiling at the memory, "but he used the wrong words, so I gently corrected him."

The linguist smiled at the memory. "He taught me how to bawl him out in his own language."

From 1962 to 1967, Domingo worked not only as a gardener for Ken, but as his formal language helper. Together they translated the TEN COMMANDMENTS, a few hymns, and the GOSPEL OF MARK into Chamula. But early in their association, despite Domingo's willingness to assist, Ken came very close to giving up and returning to the United States.

As the Jacobs discovered the alphabet, syllables, and words of the Chamula language, they also needed to tackle the more complex grammatical constructions—phrases, clauses, and sentences. The richness and incredible intricacy of this Mayan dialect became apparent and oftentimes daunting. "It was one thing to memorize a word, but quite another to understand the rules which govern the use of that word in a different grammatical setting," noted Ken.

For instance, in English and in Spanish, there are certain 'markers' that, when used in proximity to a word, identify it as either a noun or a verb. In Chamula, these markers do not necessarily appear alongside the words they identify. Without knowing the rules that govern the interplay between noun and verb markers, it was difficult to fully grasp the language. This frustrated Ken. To reach the point where he, along with a Chamula helper, could translate the Word of God accurately, Ken had to understand those rules. Despite several years of intense effort, he did not.

"All translators live by two principles—fidelity and intelligibility," said Ken. "Fidelity has to do with truth, and intelligibility has to do with under-

---

[39] Domingo would stay for days at a time in Las Casas while he worked for the Jacobs. Eventually, Ken built a simple room for Domingo inside their large walled compound, where he slept and his family could stay when they came to visit him.

standing. When a Maya Indian hears MATTHEW 5:3 in his own language,[40] it must be accurate. He must hear exactly what God is saying to him and nothing else. That's fidelity. But the only way he will comprehend what is being said will be to hear it clearly in his own language. That is intelligibility."[41]

It is crucial that a translator have a good grasp of the grammar before any Scriptural translation begins. "I didn't have to be a good speaker of the language," Ken added, "but I had to be able to understand its grammar in order to live by those two principles, and for the longest time, I couldn't."

It was a barrier that Ken's language helper could not breach for him. The Chamulas themselves could not articulate the rules of their own language. Until the Jacobs arrived, the language had never been reduced to writing, nor had it ever been formally taught in a classroom. The dialect's unwritten rules were passed on to succeeding generations simply through daily use.

Domingo could speak his language with expertise, but he could not adequately explain to his employer and friend the code governing its use. The moment Ken violated one of these rules, however, Domingo could readily point it out. The process of learning the Chamula grammar was one of exploring and probing for the unwritten rules. So far, many of these rules had eluded Ken.

Early in his association with the Jacobs, Domingo traveled with Ken and Elaine to attend an SIL language workshop at Ixmiquilpan *(eesh • mee • keel • pahn)* in the central Mexican state of Hidalgo. Here, Ken was asked to write a grammatical statement on the Chamula language. Try as he might, he could not. "I never told anybody at the time," recalls Ken years later, "but secretly I would have welcomed any excuse, like the illness of a family member or the lack of financial support, to give up and go home to the United States."

While at Ixmiquilpan, the Jacobs stayed in a duplex. Sharing the other side was an accomplished linguist, Robert Longacre.[42] Bob was engaged in translating another language dialect at the time.

One day Bob was hanging his wash out to dry when Elaine approached him and confided, "Ken is so discouraged that I think he

---

[40] The passage in the NIV reads, "Blessed are the poor in spirit, for theirs is the kingdom of heaven."

[41] *Fidelity* is the translator's responsibility, while *intelligibility* is the responsibility of the language helper.

[42] Dr. Robert E. Longacre was then the International Linguistics Consultant for the Summer Institute of Linguistics.

might give up." When Elaine explained that Ken had been unable to get a handle on Chamula grammar, Bob offered to help.

Over the next three months, Bob gave Ken many assignments in the form of words, phrases, and whole sentences which he took back to Domingo to clarify their proper use. Ken would write down Domingo's response and bring it back to Bob. With Bob's expert help, Ken grew more hopeful of cracking the complex grammatical code.

Ken readily remembers his breakthrough. Pointing to a long string of words, Bob told Ken, "Treat this all as a predicate and don't expect it to function like English. Don't expect the markers to stay on the verbs."

Hearing those words, the light suddenly clicked on for Ken. "I felt like I had been born again!" he exclaimed with deep appreciation. Ken found relief and renewed optimism for undertaking his translation task. He could move ahead with both *fidelity* and *intelligibility*.

Chamula is a language rich in verbs and almost devoid of abstract nouns. As a result, the language often brings to light important truths that an English or Spanish speaker might otherwise overlook. The reverse (back to English) rendering of a Chamula verse Ken would later translate expresses this breakthrough well: "When God's Word is clarified, it gives you information, so that even the person who is unschooled can make decisions that will benefit him."[43]

Through Bob Longacre, God mercifully supplied the information concerning *how* His Word could be clarified for the Chamula people. God then supplied this information to Ken, an otherwise despairing man who, up until that time, was unschooled in the rules needed to translate the language with fidelity and intelligibility.

Even as this barrier was wonderfully cracked open, another seemingly immutable wall loomed ahead. It would prove nearly impossible to penetrate the aggressive, tradition-bound Chamula tribe with the Scriptures once translation began—without risking death itself.

---

[43] PSALM 119:130. In the NIV this same passage reads: "The unfolding of your words gives light; it gives understanding to the simple."

7
The Impossible People

HUDSON TAYLOR, missionary to China, astutely observed that the spread of God's Word to each nation, tribe, and tongue occurs in three distinct stages: the impossible, the difficult, and the done.[44] During the late 1950s and early 1960s, the effort to acquaint Chamula Indians with the grace of God found in Jesus Christ was decidedly in stage one—the impossible stage.

The indigenous tribes of southern Mexico, with their Christo-Pagan religion and history of exploitation by the outside world, had developed powerful traditions to defend themselves and preserve their tribal identities. Many would not allow foreigners or their ideas into tribal areas. Stories abounded of outsiders living in remote areas of the Chiapas highlands who were assassinated, or tourists wandering into forbidden zones and never returning.

One similar story belongs to the Jacobs.

In 1956, before Ken and Elaine began their work with the Chamula people, the Jacobs rented a house close to territory controlled by another Tzotzil Maya Tribe, the Huistecos. A handful of Huistecos had become followers of Christ, but most of the tribe clung to their traditional animistic beliefs. Now living nearby, the Jacobs hoped to establish friendships and learn the Tzotzil Maya dialect of the Huisteco people.

Elaine and twelve-year-old daughter Joyce were home alone. Ken had gone to visit three Huisteco believers who lived twelve hours away in the Chiapas highlands. Unaware that a group of nearby Huisteco traditionalists

[44] **Leslie T. Lyall** (1965), *A Passion for the Impossible: The Continuing Story of the Mission Hudson Taylor Began* (London: OMF Books), p. 5.

were creeping toward their house under cover of a dimly lit moon, Elaine and Joyce had retired for the night. Without warning, terrifying blasts of muzzle-loaded shotguns fired at close range, directly into the walls of their home. Elaine and her daughter hugged the floor while the hit men emptied round after round of buckshot into the thick adobe walls. Leaving behind no doubt about their feelings toward the outsiders, the men quickly disappeared into the hills. Neither of them were harmed, but an Indian man from another tribe, who sought shelter that night on the Jacobs' porch, was shot and later disappeared in his own trail of blood.

Of the more than two dozen tribes which comprise the Tzotzil language group, the Chamulas were the largest. They were also the most aggressive in defending their traditions and dealt harshly with non-conformity to tribal law. The example of president-elect Sebastián Gómez Checheb—a story many mothers relayed to their children—served to drive home this point among all Chamulas.

Sebastián had been named by the ruling elders of the tribe to be their president for one year. He never became president. He became a corpse.

In casual conversation with fellow Chamulas, Sebastián suggested renting out a small piece of land near a graveyard on the outskirts of San Juan to a Ladino man who wished to farm it. "The share-crop rent would supplement our community income," Sebastián reasoned. It is one thing for a Chamula to *think* of letting in outsiders, but quite another to *talk out loud* about it. Gossip quickly passed from mouth to mouth, and the tribal elders moved into action. The council of officials, ex-officials, religious leaders, advisors, and the tribal police force all gathered to weigh Sebastián's departure from tradition.

The older men told of crooked dealings from the outside world and how that had damaged the traditions handed down by the ancestors. Younger men cited more recent examples of outside encroachment in neighboring tribes. Finally old jXantux López Oso addressed the council. *Quitsintac....* "My younger brothers." With that one expression he established his authority. He then summarized all who had spoken before him and concluded, "Sebastián Gómez Checheb carries a dangerous idea and for that he must die." No vote was taken. That was neither customary nor necessary. The council had reached a consensus.

Quietly, the authorities made plans to kill Sebastián. They concocted their trap that very afternoon. As darkness settled in a few hours later, the death squad armed themselves with machetes, pistols, and muzzle-loaded guns. They circled his home, planning to make quick work of the dissenter.

Sebastián sensed a trap. He bolted from his house, breaking through the circle of executioners with every ounce of speed he could muster. In the confusion and fear of shooting one of their own men, the killers held their fire for just an instant. That split-second hesitation was what Sebastián needed, and he bounded off unharmed into the darkness. What seemed to the elders like a fool-proof plan to kill him had failed.

Sebastián stayed away for two years, but homesickness for his family and traditions of his ancestors drew him back. "Perhaps my long absence has dulled memories," he mused. But egregious offenses like violation of tribal tradition are never forgotten. Nor are they forgiven. One day, the big Sunday crowd in the village market noticed Sebastián. So had the elders.

Someone deceptively yelled, "Fire!" At that point, tribal police arrested Sebastián on contrived charges of arson. They bound him to the large pole in the center of the plaza.

"You devils," spat Sebastián from his humiliating position. "I'd rather have the Mexicans hear my case; take me to Las Casas."

An elder retorted, "You who love the outsiders shall be taken to them. All the people shall see that they will never return you."

Having appealed to be tried by the Mexican justice system, the ex-president-elect was led by tribal police down the trail toward Las Casas; but the tribal police already had their secret orders. When out of sight from the villagers, they turned on Sebastián and viciously beat him with machetes and clubs.

As he sank to the ground in death, his twelve-year-old son climbed innocently over a ridge searching for his father. "Daddy! Daddy!" shouted the boy. Spying the body of his father, the boy came near and fell to the ground, weeping uncontrollably. The policemen glanced knowingly at each other. One necessary step in carrying out a tribal decision leads to another. The policemen's brutal black clubs quickly crushed the skull of the innocent young man. The ragged, lifeless little body rolled against that of his father.

Juan Pérez Jolote, Ken Jacob's first language helper, was one of the elders giving consent to Sebastián's murder. With this knowledge, Ken sometimes wondered how the Word of God would ever penetrate the Chamula nation. In utter frustration Ken once declared, "These stubborn Chamulas will never come to Christ." Still, the Jacobs pressed on, strengthened by their belief in the God who parted the Red Sea so the Israelites could walk across on dry land. They believed this same God was able to perform a similar miracle—one that would allow the message of forgiveness and grace safe passage across an angry sea of tribal intolerance.

BEFORE they had mastered the Chamula language, Ken and Elaine were hosting a delegation of five pastors from the United States; the pastors had come to acquaint themselves with SIL's work in southern Mexico. One morning Ken took the pastors up a mountain on the edge of San Cristóbal de Las Casas. From there the group could look across a low ridge of hills into the very heart of the Chamula tribal region. A soft haze floated across the deep valleys that morning; smoke curled up from the thatched roofed homes clinging to the steep hillsides. Ken shared his vision of bringing the Word of God to this indigenous tribe. As the men peered into these forbidden tribal lands, one pastor demanded, "What are *you* doing to evangelize the Chamulas?" Familiar with generally accepted methods of spreading the Gospel in North America, Ken recognized this was not so much a question as it was a judgmental barb meant to imply the Jacobs were not doing 'true' missionary work.

After a moment's thought, Ken replied to the man's question. "If you mean that Elaine and I are out knocking on Chamula doors," said Ken, "we'd probably get to the second house before feeling a razor-sharp machete on our necks or the blast of a muzzle-loaded gun in our backs. Or, if you mean by evangelizing the Chamulas that we set up a public address system in the center of San Juan Chamula—what an opportunity! Thousands of Chamulas attend festivals in that political and religious center. But what in the world would we say, and how would we say it?" asked Ken. "There are very few who understand Spanish, and I don't know the Chamula language yet. Even if I could speak their language, in the Chamula culture new information is never shared in public. It is confided to the most intimate friends, where you know you won't be killed for it." Ken concluded, "If that is what you mean by evangelizing the Chamulas, then Elaine and I are doing absolutely nothing."

Ken paused briefly to let the reality of his response take root. Then he continued, "There *is* a way." He explained that Chamulas need money to buy wives, to pay their liquor bills, to purchase a shaman's services, and to pay fees assessed each household for religious festivals. The corn and vegetables they grow on tribal land is often insufficient to supply these financial needs. Consequently, they temporarily leave their homes in the highlands to work in the *fincas* of the lowlands or to look for yard work in nearby Las Casas where wealthier people live.

"Elaine and I have a rather large yard with a garden, chickens, and pigs, and we could hire Chamula men looking for work. Behind the security of high walls, and over time, we could learn the language from these workers and reduce it to writing. If we can communicate with one or two, eventually we will be able to communicate with all Chamulas." Ken then added, "If, little by little, we can begin to translate the Scripture into their language and the Word of God ignites a spark of faith in the heart of just one man, and if that man, when he comes to understand the grace of God, is willing to risk his life to tell another— and he'll *have* to risk his life—then that little spark could become a flame of belief. Eventually the flame could become a fire of conviction that would spread throughout the whole tribe."[45]

MOST Chamulas did not associate with residents of Las Casas, except to supplement their limited incomes by selling home-grown produce in

---

[45] SIL's contract with the Mexican government prevented its linguists from proselytizing. Consequently, God's Word would need to be shared with Chamulas by Chamulas.

the marketplace or by working as day laborers. Ken's second language helper, Domingo Hernández Aguilar, was different. In every society, there are people on the fringe who secretly question their authorities and traditions. Domingo was such a man. He dared to entertain unconventional thoughts—and even doubts—about Chamula tradition. When a pregnant mare wandered away from his land, Domingo engaged the services of a local shaman to find her. After performing the prescribed ceremonies, including drinking the *pox*, lighting the candles, and burning the incense Domingo had purchased, the shaman confidently informed him where he could locate his horse. Domingo went looking for the mare but could not find her. Soon after, Domingo had a dream. In his dream he saw a meadow where his mare was grazing. The very next morning, Domingo walked to that meadow and found the mare. Gingerly standing alongside was her newborn foal.

This situation and other negative experiences served to bolster Domingo's skepticism of his tribe's traditional beliefs—even to the point where he spoke contemptuously of the shaman's failure to locate his horse. "You'd better be careful what you say," warned his wife, Verónica, who was a practicing shaman herself. She knew all too well the penalty for questioning Chamula tribal and religious authorities. But Domingo would not be dissuaded from criticizing, at least in private, a system he viewed as flawed.

It came as no surprise that Domingo agreed to help the Jacobs advance their understanding of the Chamula language. A more timid person might have shied away from such close association with outsiders. Yet there were times when Domingo became uneasy at what he was hearing. As he helped Ken translate some hymns, then the TEN COMMANDMENTS, then record a few Bible stories on vinyl discs, Domingo wondered to himself, "What will the tribal authorities say if they hear my voice on some of the recordings we are making?"

Ken was worried he'd lose Domingo. For less serious infractions, other Chamula men had watched helplessly as tribally-sanctioned mobs burned their houses, burned their crops, and threatened their families with physical harm. But Domingo stayed on. He even brought his brother-in-law, Miguel, a former shaman, into the Jacobs' two-and-a-half-acre yard to help care for their animals.

When Ken and his helper had drafted the GOSPEL OF MARK (the first NEW TESTAMENT book translated into the Chamula language), Ken invited Domingo to accompany him back to SIL's language workshop in Ixmiquilpan. This time he wanted Domingo to check the quality of the translation with Biblical scholars. But Domingo was preoccupied with a problem at home. The mud-covered wooden walls of his family's house had rotted out and were now collapsing. "How can I go with you when my house is falling down?" he asked Ken. Domingo had propped up the walls with poles, but he was fearful a strong wind might bring the crumbling structure down on his family. He needed money and time to build a new house. So Ken offered to loan him the money. Soon after he rebuilt his house, Domingo joined Ken in Ixmiquilpan.

Returning afterward to Las Casas, the Jacobs had cause for celebration. The scholars had approved their translation of MARK, with but few revisions. It was already scheduled to be published. Meanwhile Domingo returned to a newly reconstructed home. A few days later, when working with Ken at their translation desk, Domingo asked, "What kind of ceremony would you and Elaine hold if you built a new house?" Domingo explained that in the Chamula religious system, a new house is considered vulnerable to evil spirits. Traditionalists conduct a series of rituals to ward off these spirits. The rituals include burying heads of chickens under the corner posts of the new house and making a special soup to pour over the rafters. "I don't want to do that!" announced Domingo, and again he asked Ken the same question.

Ken could not think of how to explain a dedication service, so he simply told Domingo, "We give the house to God."

"That's what I want to do," declared Domingo, insisting that Ken and Elaine come to a celebration at his new home. There was only one problem. Domingo's house was located in a village immediately adjacent to the tribe's political and ceremonial center, San Juan Chamula.

"They don't want us out there," protested Ken, reflecting on the danger to any outsider who dares to venture into Chamula territory—not to mention the hazard to the Chamula person who invites him.

"Who are *they*?" countered Domingo with a grin on his face and a tinge of contempt in his voice. "It's *my* house, and I can do what I please. I'm asking you to come."

To avoid suspicious eyes, the Jacobs departed Las Casas after sunset. The path ahead was dark. Clouds obscured the moon and no street-lights illumined the narrow rural road. As they began the winding climb into the highlands north of the city, Ken switched off their 1958 Chevy's headlights. The boundaries of the gravel grade were barely visible as the '58 climbed the slope towards San Juan Chamula.

While Ken strained to see ahead, Elaine and Jerry,[46] the couple's six-year-old adopted son, quietly surveyed the dark night. Occasionally they glimpsed a flicker of light as the car passed one of the thatched roof huts. Throughout the approximately 30-mile by 30-mile territory of Chamula, huts were grouped into ninety villages blanketing Chamula's nearly 1,000 square miles of mountainous terrain.

Chamulas constructed their huts by lashing sticks together and covering them with mud to form walls. The average home was a 10' by 10' structure with a bath house on the side (Chamulas bathe with steam generated by pouring cold water over hot rocks). A cornfield adjoined each hut.

The dried corn stalks gave a Halloween-like atmosphere to the countryside as the outsiders drove higher, penetrating deep into forbidden territory. Although most huts were not visible from the road, the Jacobs could smell them as they drove by. Each gave off the distinct odor of ground corn. Each hut also emitted a plume of smoke, vented between the walls and the roof from a fire in the center of the hut. The fire occasionally smolders from green wood used for fuel, but never goes out completely.

Though the outsiders maintained their silence, the higher up the mountain they drove, the more Ken and Elaine came to grips with the risk they were taking. Persuaded by amiable Domingo to witness a celebration at his new home, maybe they'd too eagerly put aside their fears

---

[46] During their twenty-five years in San Cristóbal de Las Casas, Elaine Jacobs helped find homes for many orphaned or abandoned children, both Indian and Ladino. One was a baby boy whom the Jacobs themselves adopted and named Jerry.

when they agreed to this precarious late-night excursion. They knew from previous experience they were not welcome. On an earlier trip to San Juan Chamula, in broad daylight, unseen hands had lobbed stones at their car, despite having a respected tribal elder in their passenger seat. On this pitch-black night, they had no such advocate with them.

Ken experienced a deep sense of foreboding as he drove Elaine and Jerry to the party. "We just don't belong here," he thought, his mind racing, his eyes scanning the darkness ahead. "Nothing good can come of this." Every hut they passed belonged to someone who was not their friend.

The route to Domingo's home took the Jacobs around one side of the historic church and plaza located in the heart of San Juan Chamula. Constructed in Spanish colonial times, the church was Catholic in name only. With the exception of occasional baptisms performed by a visiting priest, the building was now used primarily for pagan rituals and festivals. Draped in white cloth, the cross on which young Domingo Gómez Checheb had been crucified in 1868 was still prominently, reverently displayed inside. Nervously, the Jacobs drove around the building. Climbing the last few hundred yards to the top of a hill behind the old church, Ken brought the car to a stop at Domingo's house. It looked deserted.

Suddenly, the doors of their Chevy flew open, pulled outward by unseen forces. Unidentified hands wasted no time extracting the horrified family from the relative safety of their car and into the inky blackness of the night.

8
Night Of Joy And Terror

"**H**ERMANO!" "*HERMANA!*" shouted the Jacobs' abductors. Mercifully, these Spanish terms for *brother* and *sister* identified the hands as friends. In fact, the hands pulling the Jacobs into the shrouded night belonged to other guests at Domingo's celebration. Reassuring voices guided Ken, Elaine, and Jerry—still a bit shaken—along the last few feet of path in the brisk December darkness. Moments later a warm, beckoning light greeted them as the door to their language helper's new home swung open, revealing a blazing cooking fire in the center of the room. The trio edged closer to the fire, awestruck at the bright faces of new Chamula friends who, only moments earlier, had tempered their fears by calling them brother and sister.

The celebration that followed had been planned by Domingo from beginning to end. In every aspect it was a dedication of his house to the author of the *Good New Words* which he and Ken were translating. The little group sang JESUS LOVES ME; they recited both the LORD'S PRAYER and the TEN COMMANDMENTS—all in the Chamula language. They listened intently while Bible stories spoken in their native tongue—like THE LOST SHEEP, THE PRODIGAL SON, and THE GOOD SHEPHERD—sprang forth from the speakers of a record player without the aid of electricity. Domingo simply rotated the disk with his index finger at just the right speed.

At some point in the festivities, it dawned on Ken and Elaine that they were witnessing perhaps the first Christian worship service ever to be held within Chamula tribal territory. A flame of faith had finally been ignited, piercing generations of crushing spiritual darkness. Tiny grains of *Good New Words* had been sprinkled like yeast into the consciousness of this indigenous people—not only by the Jacobs, but by other believers God had used over the years. But it wasn't until this crisp December evening in the heart of Chamula territory that a handful of Chamula people finally gathered together as the first fruits of God's transforming grace.

GOD'S Word had been introduced into the Mexican State of Chiapas in the late 1800s. Christians from Guatemala and itinerate Bible salesmen brought Spanish-language versions of the Bible into the lowland coffee growing areas of the state. The first known believer from Chiapas lived on a *finca* near the city of Tapachula in 1878.

Early in the Twentieth Century, several small groups of Ladino believers were meeting throughout the state. They began taking God's Word to the more receptive Indian tribes in the Chiapan highlands. The first believers in the Ch'ol[47] language group were baptized in the 1920s. By 1931, a Ladino congregation known as the *Church of the Divine Redeemer* was organized in San Cristóbal de Las Casas under the auspices of the Mexican Presbyterian Church.[48]

A few decades later—but prior to the dedication of his new house—these influences converged during a providential conversation on the value of education between Domingo Hernández Aguilar and a Ladino mason. Domingo was helping the mason lay bricks in the Jacobs' Las Casas yard. Convinced that Domingo would benefit from additional schooling, the mason introduced Domingo to a Ch'ol man, Cristóbal Trujillo. "I attend a night school here in Las Casas from 7:00 P.M. to 9:00 P.M.," Cristóbal informed Domingo. "Would you like to attend with me?"

Unlike most in his tribe, Domingo already spoke some Spanish. He'd gained a basic understanding of the language by working along-

---

[47] **Ch'ol** — one of five Mayan languages actively spoken in Chiapas. The other four are Tzotzil, Tzeltal, Tojolobal, and Lacandon. Chamula is a dialect of Tzotzil.

[48] This brief history of Christianity's development in Chiapas comes from the author's personal conversations with Alan John Schreuder, Reformed Church of America Missionary to the Tzotzil Presbytery of the National Presbyterian Church of Mexico since 1980. Al is also an instructor in church history and theology at the Tzotzil Bible Institute.

side Ladinos in the *fincas*. He had also completed three years of education in a government sponsored tribal school in San Juan Chamula. This brief exposure to Spanish enabled Domingo to communicate with, and to assist, Ken Jacobs as Ken worked to master the Chamula language. But it also left Domingo with a desire to know more. "I would like to go back to school," he told Cristóbal, and the two men, from two different tribes, began attending night school together.

One evening as they walked back to the Jacobs' compound, Cristóbal asked Domingo, "What is your religion—what do you believe?"

"Well, I consider myself a Catholic and our patron saint is San Juan," said Domingo. He gave Cristóbal all the details he could remember about the veneration of the plaster saints lining the walls of his church, and about fearing the nature gods that form the basis of the Chamulas' worldview. In the end he admitted, "I really don't know much about that religion, and I hardly ever go to church."

His Ch´ol schoolmate replied, "You need to know the real, true God. I'd be glad to tell you about Him, if you really want to know."

Domingo had heard a little of this God from men working in the *fincas*. He wasn't interested then, and he wasn't all that interested now, as he told his friend. "Well," said Cristóbal, "at least let me give you a Spanish NEW TESTAMENT and then you can read about it on your own, whenever you want to." Though he still could not read Spanish very well, Domingo accepted the gift; it was a way to practice the Spanish he was learning in night school.

A few weeks later, Cristóbal invited Domingo to attend worship services at the *Church of the Divine Redeemer* in Las Casas. At first Domingo resisted. He would feel awkward with all those Ladinos staring at him. But his Ch´ol friend persisted. "They're not people who will look down on you," he said. "The people there will accept you." So the Ch´ol and Chamula men established a Sunday custom. Cristóbal would come over to the Jacobs' compound where Domingo was staying, and the two men would walk to the church. Domingo found the worship services surprisingly interesting. He couldn't understand everything that went on, but afterwards, Cristóbal would explain what the message was about and what had taken place.

One day Cristóbal asked Domingo, "Have you ever read JOHN 3:16[49] and thought about what it says?" His Ch´ol friend read the passage and Domingo replied,

"I've heard before that everyone has to account for their sins."

"But this is good news," said Cristóbal. "JOHN 3:16 says you don't have to pay for your sins. They're already paid for by Jesus, who died in your place, so that God will accept you."

While working on the NEW TESTAMENT translation with Ken Jacobs, Domingo had met Indians, including Tzotzils like himself, who recommended this God. One day, a Huisteco[50] Tzotzil named Nicolás came to the Jacobs' compound and told Domingo he should take seriously the work he was doing with Ken. "I was a killer, a liquor maker, a robber, and a wife beater," he told the Chamula. "But God's Word made me what I am today—a changed person." Domingo was deeply impressed.

The more Domingo thought about these things and the more he attended church, the better God's Word sounded to him. One day he told Cristóbal, "I've decided to become a believer." Though serious about his decision, Domingo did not talk to anyone else about it. But he did decide it was time to learn more about this God, so he began reading his Spanish Bible in earnest.

The Jacobs noticed an unmistakable change in their language helper. Early in 1963 Ken Jacobs wrote to his supporters that "Domingo has begun talking favorably to me about what we believe. Even his attitude toward translation changed." Previously Domingo had sometimes expressed reluctance about translating the Bible because of the personal risk involved. Now Ken noted, "He is a reliable helper and has told me he is going to stay on. Consequently, we are aiming at finishing the BOOK OF MARK by the end of February."

After several months, Domingo began telling those closest to him about the God who saves. He traveled home to Chamula and told his wife, Verónica, what he was reading in the Bible. "Do you want to

---

[49] "For God so loved the world that he gave his one and only Son, that whoever believes in him shall not perish but have eternal life" (NIV).

[50] **Huistecos** — one of more than two dozen Tzotzil Indian tribes. The Jacobs originally began their translation work among the Tzotzil Huisteco people, prior to their work among the Tzotzil Chamula people; *cf.* Chapter 7.

believe, too?" he asked her.

"Well, I don't know," countered his wife, a practicing shaman. "Tell me more about this."

"When you go to the Catholic Church in San Juan Chamula and you see Christ hanging on the cross," he began, "that is not the real Christ."

"What do you mean?" she asked. "There's an image there—I can see it."

"What I mean is this," continued Domingo. "A long time ago, there was a living man named Jesus. He was a real person, not just an image. He died on a real cross and paid for our sins." Domingo explained that God will grant anyone who believes in Jesus and his *Good New Words* eternal life in heaven.

"That sounds good to me," said Verónica, who was intimately familiar with the hopeless cycle of life and death in the Chamula tradition.

Domingo's brother-in-law, Miguel, who had also heard the Gospel proclaimed while working in the *fincas*, joined Domingo in rejecting the traditional beliefs of their tribe to follow the God of the Bible. The two families began meeting together in Domingo's house to study God's Word. Located in the village of Vinik Ton, just above the famed church of San Juan Chamula, this assembly provided the first Christian witness in that tribe of what was then 35,000 people.

So it was that Ken and Elaine, in late 1963, found themselves in an unexpected but delightful worship service with the first Chamulas to embrace the *Good New Words*. The Jacobs played no role in that worship service. The Chamulas did everything, including serving a savory meal of chicken soup with plenty of beans, tortillas, and soda pop. As if to underline the new authority to which this fledging group had pledged their allegiance, the sugar cane liquor *pox* that accompanied most Chamula celebrations was noticeably absent.

Despite the festive occasion, the Jacobs' hosts were visibly nervous throughout the celebration. From time to time they would push open the door of the house and peer intently into the darkness, alert to any movement that might indicate someone was watching their gathering. At 2:00 A.M., with Jerry already dozing on Elaine's lap, the Jacobs excused themselves and climbed back into their car for the long ride down the gravel grade to Las Casas.

Ken didn't want to attract attention on the way down the mountain, any more than on the way up. He kept the lights and engine off while the Chevy coasted down the first steep hill and entered San Juan Chamula. Approaching the ancient Spanish church from the rear, Ken turned the key in the ignition and the engine jumped to life. Shifting into second gear, he switched on the headlights. There in the high beams heading straight up the road toward their car was a band of Chamula traditionalists carrying torches and machetes. There appeared to be no way to avoid this human roadblock.

"Ken, Ken, turn!" cried Elaine, alert to the fact that they had reached a crossroad. Ken yanked the wheel sharply left and sped down an old road on the opposite side of the church. The mob had expected them to take the newer road on the right. Ken and Elaine breathed a sigh of relief, but only for a moment. Their hearts sank as the horde turned and strode quickly across the plaza in front of the church, aiming to intersect their new course. Would the mob reach the old road in time to block their path? With the exit from that dark town close in sight, Ken jammed the accelerator to the floor. In seconds, the Chevy slipped past the mob and roared down the road until the torches were merely pinpoints in the rearview mirror.

"The only danger now," Ken said to Elaine, "is if they have the road to Las Casas blocked with tree trunks or rocks." It wasn't. But what would become of their friends back at Domingo's house? The Jacobs worried these new believers might be attacked or killed.

9
Bridges Of Belief

SOME SOCIETIES are like onions. Peel back the skin, and you discover several layers underneath. One layer is business. One is government. Another, social relationships. Still another is religion. Though related, these layers are usually separate and distinct.

Chamula society is more like an apple. It's the same from just below the surface all the way to the core. Beneath a protective skin of isolation, traditional religious beliefs permeate every conceivable aspect of Chamula life, from law and commerce to marriage and family. Everything—even succession of tribal leadership or the proper way to dedicate a house—has to do with the gods. There is no exception. Domingo's decision to dedicate his recently-constructed home to a new deity, the author of the *Good New Words*, was dangerous. Ramifications of his decision would affect *every* aspect of his life, and according to tribal elders, the very well-being of his community.

Little wonder the first believers were wary of their neighbors, expecting at any moment to fend off severe opposition to their new beliefs. After their close encounter with the horde of torch-bearing Chamula traditionalists, it would not have surprised the Jacobs to hear that the families of Domingo and his friends had been attacked, burned out, beaten, jailed—or worse. Fortunately, for the time being, they appeared to have been overlooked.

Around 10:00 A.M. the next morning Domingo's wife, Verónica, knocked at the Jacobs' gate. Elaine welcomed her graciously, but quickly inquired, "Did anyone visit your home after we left last night?"

"We saw no one," replied Verónica.

Elaine breathed a quick prayer of thanks. Then she described to the Chamula woman in detail their narrow escape from the traditionalists.

These first Chamula believers did not experience open persecution right away. They appear to have been supernaturally protected for a period of time—empowered to spread the transforming message to others in the tribe. Nonetheless, it was apparent the elders were watching.

Back to the apple: a biological organism usually invades an apple from one of two directions. It either enters at a point in the skin and moves toward the core, or it begins at the core and moves outward toward the skin. The enzyme of the Gospel entered Chamula in both directions. The first believers lived in a village, Vinik Ton, very near the core of Chamula's political and ceremonial center. It spread from there to villages on the farthest perimeters of the 1,000-square-mile tribal territory. But the Chamula people propagating this Word were living 'on the skin'—the extreme edge of Chamula society. They were individuals who had run afoul of the traditional belief system and were questioning its validity. Others soon joined them.

᭜ ᭜ ᭜ ☥ ? ? ?

TWENTY-year-old Manuel Caxtuli stared hard at the ground as he sat next to his younger brother, Tumin, on a long wooden bench in front of the *cabildo* of San Juan Chamula. Tribal president Domingo Lunes Ch´akil Chij had summoned both men to a meeting with the *moletique (mol•e•teek•ey)*—the wise people, the perpetuators of tradition who act as judges in deciding the most serious matters facing tribal leadership. The presence of *mayols* (tribal policemen) on the left and right of Manuel and Tumin identified the brothers as the serious matter facing the council that evening.

At issue was the well-known fact that an increasing number of these young men's relatives, neighbors, and friends were meeting at Manuel's house in the village of Nich´en, not far from San Juan

Chamula. They were studying a strange new belief. At first the tribal leadership had expressed little concern about reports from local watchdogs: handfuls of their countrymen were assembling each Sunday to study and discuss the outsiders' Bible, parts of which were rumored to have been printed recently in a version more easily understood by Chamula speakers.

When these Sunday morning meetings first began in 1964, the tribal president had been Salvador Sántiz Diezmo. "I already know about your meetings," he told Manuel and Tumin, when the brothers felt compelled to inform Salvador of their weekly activities. "It's not a problem." But disinterest gave way to disapproval when the tribal council appointed Domingo Lunes as president the following year. By that time there were people coming to the brothers' Sunday morning gatherings from the villages of Joltsemen and Sactzu, each making the seven or eight-hour roundtrip walk.

Domingo Lunes met Manuel on the trail one day and asked him if it was really true they were worshipping a god different than those prescribed by Chamulas' ancestors. When Manuel confirmed it, the president told Manuel that some of the people in his village might not like that. "You're a good friend of mine and I don't want you to get into trouble with your neighbors," he said, laying groundwork for the proposition he was about to make. "How about if you stop having those meetings? You don't have to go back to our traditional beliefs. I'll keep quiet about this and try to protect you."

"No," replied Manuel. "Other people want to know about the God of the Bible and want to believe, too. It's not something I can stop talking about."

"Okay, if that's the way you want to be. I can't guarantee your safety." As the tribal official moved down the trail, he tossed another warning over his shoulder: "There's no telling what people might wind up doing if you continue to meet."

In the weeks following that encounter nothing serious occurred. Manuel fielded the usual questions and comments from his neighbors in Nich´en. Some were guardedly curious. Others had difficulty disguising their distain for this new belief being so openly practiced in a society where the prescribed religion was rigidly guarded. Nothing ominous had occurred—until this afternoon's unexpected arrival at Manuel's house of two *mayols* charged with escorting Manuel and his brother Tumin to the *cabildo*.

AS he sat waiting apprehensively on the bench, Manuel Caxtuli remembered the first time he heard about this new God. He'd been wrestling with an addiction to alcohol that was keeping his family in perpetual poverty, and his uncle, Miguel Cashlan, had spoken with him. "You are drinking much and always getting drunk," his uncle observed. "Give it up and put your trust in the words of the Lord Jesus Christ, who can deliver you from your life of alcoholism."

Miguel Gómez Chakojchu (his uncle's actual name) had recently been delivered from many of the same demons troubling Manuel. He'd been orphaned soon after birth and was raised by another relative. At age ten he found a way to escape the ever-present hunger and conflict engulfing his surrogate home. Miguel enrolled as an intern in the only community school in Chamula. One day a European visiting the school saw Miguel's ragged clothing and gave him a shirt, pants, and shoes. Now stigmatized for wearing Spanish-style clothes, he was nicknamed Miguel Cashlan (Miguel the Outsider).

Miguel proved a good student. He continued his studies, eventually attending a school near the state capital, Tuxtla Gutierrez, and later in Mexico City. He gained a good understanding of Spanish and of the Mexican constitution. Despite some success, he experienced prejudice in the Ladino world and remained an outsider in that culture. Poor health forced his return to Chamula, where he farmed and worked for a while as a shaman, but was no good at either. Occupational failures and personal failures in family and public life left him as an outsider within Chamula as well.[51]

[51] Information in the preceding two paragraphs was derived from **Gary H. Gossen** (1989), *Life, Death, and Apotheosis of a Chamula Protestant Leader: Biography as Social History*, as cited in: **V. R. Bricker** & **G. H. Gossen** (1989), *Ethnographic Encounters in Mesoamerica: Essays in Honor of Evon Zartman Vogt, Jr.* (Albany NY: Institute for Mesoamerican Studies, Albany State University of New York).

After abandoning his second wife, Miguel spent many years in the lowland coffee *fincas*. It was there he heard the Gospel for the first time. Not until much later, feeling the pain of rejection and sinking deeper into alcoholism, did Miguel begin to take seriously the Word of God. At that point he and his brother-in-law, Domingo Hernández Aguilar, began meeting regularly at Domingo's home in Vinik Ton to study what it meant to live by the words of this new deity. Domingo, too, was Manuel Caxtuli's uncle.

Miguel had several conversations with his nephew Manuel before inviting him to meet with the others who were beginning to believe. Manuel told his wife Juana, "I am hearing from Miguel that we can find freedom from the way we're living if we begin to put our trust in the words of this new God." The couple decided to attend the gathering in Domingo's home the very next Sunday.

Manuel and Juana listened carefully to the teaching, and to claims by Miguel and Domingo that Manuel could be delivered from his alcoholism. At one point, uncertain of this new power but desperate for a solution, Manuel broke down and wept. "If you turn your life over to the work of Christ, you will find deliverance," urged Miguel.

As the day ended, Manuel and Juana headed home. On the way, they reviewed what they had heard concerning Jesus' words in the GOSPEL OF MARK. "I tell you the truth, if anyone says to this mountain, 'Go throw yourself into the sea,' and does not doubt in his heart, but believes that what he says will happen, it will be done for him."[52] The couple marveled at promises like this and the hope such promises offered. Together they decided to believe, and that very evening began to experience freedom. Manuel in particular was delivered from his desire for alcohol.

GRATEFUL for their newfound freedom, Manuel and Juana followed Jesus' instructions to "Go home to your family and tell them how much the Lord has done for you, and how he has had mercy on you."[53] The

---

[52] MARK 11:23/NIV.

[53] Jesus' words after healing the demon-possessed man from Gadarenes (MARK 5:19/NIV).

first person Manuel spoke to was his brother Tumin.

Tumin Caxtuli had often been sick while growing up. As a young man of sixteen, and newly married to María, his illness had returned. It was compounded by a growing addiction to alcohol. When he drank, Tumin became wild. In fits of alcoholic rage he beat his wife and other family members.

He consulted one shaman after another, trying to find relief from his maladies. Each one, after checking Tumin's blood and performing other diagnostic rituals, told him the same thing. "You're going to die; but first, you'll go crazy and they'll tie you to a tree to keep you from injuring yourself or others," the shamans predicted. Tumin was depressed—but his brother's recent encounter with a different power offered the tiniest prospect of escape from a dreadful end.

"I've got hope for you," said Manuel one day. "If you believe in Jesus Christ, he can save you and free you from your sickness."

Manuel advised his brother to talk with Miguel. So one Sunday afternoon Tumin sought out his uncle who was selling fruits and vegetables in the marketplace at San Juan Chamula. "Is it really true?" Tumin asked. "Is there a God who can heal me?" His uncle confirmed it was true.

"If you read the Bible, it tells how God healed those with grave illnesses like leprosy and epilepsy," said Miguel. "He healed them all, but you have to believe in this God and in his son, Jesus."

That news gave Tumin hope. But his uncle continued, "I know all about you and what you're like," said Miguel. "You go to the *fincas* and work really hard, but you come home and spend all your money on liquor and beat your wife and your family. God can heal you from that, too." Tumin went home and told his wife María. Together they decided to believe, and they began to experience the healing promised by God's Word. The following Sunday the young couple walked to Vinik Ton to attend the worship service in Domingo's house.

"This is *good news* we've been given," Miguel told those assembled. "It's not enough just to believe and keep it to yourself. God will call you to tell other people about this, too." And tell they did, first to extended family and soon to friends in nearby villages.

ONE day Domingo hopped aboard a pickup for a ride into San Cristóbal. In the back of the pickup, also doubling as a local bus, he saw his close friend, Salvador Hernández Me´chij. Salvador lived in another *paraje* a short distance from Domingo's home in Vinik Ton. Though not related, Domingo's mother had worked for Salvador's family for many years, so the two had grown up together.

"Where are you going?" Domingo inquired of the friend who was practically his brother.

"To meet a shaman. While I was working on the *finca*, I got really sick," Salvador explained. "I've visited many shamans, but none has been able to cure me. I'm afraid I'm going to die. I'm on the way to see another one right now." Then Salvador asked whether Domingo's wife, Verónica, would perform a healing ceremony, if this next shaman was unable to heal him.

"You don't have to do that to be healed," Domingo blurted out, adding that his wife no longer worked as a shaman. With other ears on the bus suddenly attentive, Domingo told his friend about the *Good New Words* that he and Verónica had heard and chosen to believe. "The God who spoke those words will help you," he concluded. "He will save you, and he will make both your body and your soul well again."

That sounded appealing to Salvador, who had sold his only horse and spent nearly all of his money on traditional curing ceremonies. But he had already agreed to meet the shaman. "I don't want to trick the *j´ilol* by not showing up," said the sick man. Pondering just a bit, he added, "If this doesn't work, I want to hear more." The friends parted, and Salvador continued to his rendezvous with the shaman. This shaman also failed to achieve a cure, so Salvador returned to talk with Domingo. The next day, Sunday, Salvador brought his entire family to the worship service in Domingo's house. Salvador soon became the next Chamula to believe.

MANUEL and Tumin also found opportunities to share the new hope they had been given. As they told more acquaintances about their allegiance to the God with the *Good New Words*, the number of people meeting in Domingo's house increased. Manuel Caxtuli eventually opened his home in Nich´en to his relatives, neighbors, and friends who were beginning to believe. Occasionally the growing band of Chamula believers walked fifteen miles to San Cristóbal to Ken and Elaine Jacobs' spacious walled yard. There Domingo Hernández Aguilar and Miguel Cashlan taught the new believers and led them in worship.

The Gospel spread outward, beginning with a small nucleus of Chamulas who chose to believe. It spread within this closed society, crossing natural bridges of relationship[54] from relative to relative, from friend to friend. It even spread across bridges of common experience— illness, drunkenness, and spiritual hopelessness. When persecution arose, the suffering that resulted served as yet another bridge to spread this new way of believing and living.

MANUEL'S thoughts were interrupted by the voice of a third *mayol* who had emerged from the *cabildo*. "The elders are assembled. Come in." Still flanked by the two policemen who brought them to San Juan Chamula from Nich´en, Manuel and Tumin rose from the bench and entered the *cabildo*. As their eyes adjusted to the darkened room, the brothers were able to make out a large wooden desk in the middle of the room, with rows of chairs on either side. Occupying these chairs were the *moletique*, and behind the desk sat the president, Domingo Lunes. He rose as the Caxtuli brothers approached.

"Uncles, we have come," said Manuel, respectfully addressing the tribal leaders. It was the beginning of a formal greeting which precedes any meeting between Chamulas.

---

[54] **Alan John Schreuder** (June 2001), *A History of the Rise of the Chamula Church*—Master's Thesis (Pasadena CA: Fuller Theological Seminary, School of World Mission and Institute of Church Growth), pp. 57–59.

"Why have you come?" replied the president.

"You know why we have come," responded Manuel, politely. "You asked us."

With a grand gesture toward the Caxtuli brothers, the president addressed the wise men of the tribe. "These are the ones who are meeting together, discussing what they call the 'New Words' and talking to others about it, and this is a leader of the group," said Domingo Lunes, pointing to Manuel.

One of the elders rose. "Is it true that you have been reading these New Words?"

"Yes, my uncle," replied Manuel.

"Is it true that you are meeting together and inviting others to meet with you?" inquired the older man.

"Yes, it is true," admitted Manuel.

The questions intensified. "Well then, why are you doing this? Why are you believing in this way and disrespecting the cultures and traditions of San Juan Chamula?" asked another elder.

"I'm believing because God has spoken to me," responded Manuel.

"Who do you think you are that God would speak to you?" came the indignant reply. No longer wanting for a response, the miffed elder launched into a lecture. "You are just a kid. You're not very smart yet. Why would God reveal himself to you? Why would God talk to you about what he thinks or what he is saying?"

The *moletique* asked many more questions of Manuel and Tumin during the hour-long interrogation. Whichever brother gave the answer, those asking became even angrier. Every question became an accusation, and every answer was taken by the elders as a sign of disrespect. "You've got to stop believing," they ordered. "You've got to go back to the old ways."

"We can't go back," insisted Manuel and Tumin, trying to remain polite, and yet determined to stand their ground. "This is what God has taught us, and we need to continue saying what God wants us to say."

Finally Mol Portillo, the old man who was *alcalde* (mayor) that year, rose to speak. Instantly the room grew still. "We've heard this 'word' before, and this is not part of our tradition," he said sternly. "You must forget what you have heard and turn back to the ways of your ancestors, or you will wish you had." The old man paused for effect, then continued in a softer but slightly sinister tone. "There were others who prayed and believed what you believe," he began vaguely, as if searching his memory for an image long forgotten. His eyes brightened as the image grew clearer in his mind. "Ah, yes. Now I remember. We took them to Biq´uit Tuxtla to get rid of them."

Biq´uit Tuxtla was a large pit not far from San Juan Chamula where the tribe's artisans excavated a special clay called *chuchulumtic*, used to fabricate heavy griddles for cooking tortillas. The 'pray-ers' as Mol Portillo described them were arrested in the town square because they were not following the traditional tribal religion. "We took them to Biq´uit Tuxtla," repeated the old man, slowing his delivery and annunciating each word for emphasis. "We killed them there and threw their bodies into the pit," he added.

The room was deadly silent.

After what seemed like an eternity, the president spoke once more. "You may leave now," he ordered the brothers. "This is the end of it."

10
You Are Dead Men

THE FIRST Chamulas to embrace the *Good New Words* found themselves struggling with something more than a highly resistant traditional religious system. Their newfound faith also jeopardized personal interests of their tribal leaders who held great religious, political, and economic power.

In 1936, the Mexican government had asked all highland tribes to appoint young, bilingual men to serve on federal committees dealing with land reform, labor, and Indian affairs. Officially referred to as 'scribes,' their stated job was to record and communicate proceedings to their monolingual tribal elders. Unofficially, the young men were also given, and readily assumed, additional authority inside and outside of the tribe. Eventually the scribes asked for religious offices as well, paving their way to become elders—the respected tribal leaders. Having consolidated both civil and religious command, scribes soon became the most influential members of the tribe.

By the 1950s and 1960s, these *caciques (kah•see•kays)*, or tribal bosses, had amassed great wealth through their powerful positions within the tribes and through their connections with the outside Ladino world. They held a virtual monopoly on money lending, transportation, soda pop, liquor, candles, and other supplies necessary for religious rituals and celebrations. They exercised autocratic control over the lives of tribal members through their governmental and religious offices, occupied or filled with family members. The *cacique* had power to elevate those who pleased them and performed their will; they had power to repress those who opposed their public policies or private pursuits. The state and federal government depended on *caciques* to deliver the Indian vote and to keep peace. In exchange, government officials looked the other way as *caciques* did whatever they pleased within their highland empires.

The handful of Chamulas beginning to live the life prescribed by the God of the Bible attracted the attention of the *caciques* for several reasons. Aversion to alcohol cut liquor revenues; refusal to pursue traditional medicine affected money lending and candle sales. Some new believers refused to pay the per-family traditional religious festival assessment. This affected the *caciques'* wallets as suppliers to those festivals, and it undermined their power to tax. Perhaps most troubling was the adherence of Chamula Christians to a new religious authority— an authority the tribal bosses did not represent. They no longer had direct coercive influence over their citizens. As Chamulas' leading civic and religious leaders, the *caciques* could, however, compel the community-at-large to pressure non-conformists to conform, or pressure the community to purge the contamination. Their pretext was this: nonconformity would result in catastrophe for the whole tribe.[55]

Q'UIN Carnival, an event comparable to Mardi Gras, was a three- to four-day Chamula celebration just prior to Lent. It marked religious officials accepting or leaving office. It was also an excuse for gross misbehavior and for purging the tribe of members who refused to observe Chamula traditions. In the days leading up to the 1965 Carnival, each adult known to frequent worship services at Domingo Hernández Aguilar's house was brought before the tribal president, Domingo Lunes, and the *moletique*. This would have been six families representing about thirty men, women, and children.

Tribal leaders began by questioning the men. Besides Salvador Hernández Me´chij and the Caxtuli brothers, the elders recognized one of their own: Sebastián Hernández Caxtuli. The father of Manuel and Tumin, Sebastián was also Domingo Hernández Aguilar's brother-in-law. When Manuel believed, he spoke with his father about the *Good New*

[55] **Jan Rus** (2005), "The Struggle Against Indigenous Caciques in Highland Chiapas: Dissent, Religion and Exile in Chamula, 1965–1977," *Catiquismo in Twentieth Century Mexico* (Institute for the Americas), pp. 169–180.

Words that had transformed his life. He encouraged his father to give up drinking *pox* and to believe. Sebastián, who had recently completed a two-year-long religious *cargo*,[56] had many questions for Manuel. "Why do you want to stop drinking *pox*, which the gods gave us as a gift? Why do you want to leave the traditions of our elders? Where do these *new words* come from?" As a young believer, Manuel struggled to answer these questions, but at least his father listened. Meanwhile, Manuel's mother was intrigued by the *new words* she heard and by the positive change she saw in her son. She decided to believe, and eventually Sebastián likewise placed his faith in Christ. When Sebastián—a respected elder—was brought before the *moletique*, his confession of freedom from liquor and sin was a strong point in favor of the Christians.

Next, Domingo Lunes asked the women why they believed. Each told how their husbands used to drink and beat them, and how they stopped these abuses soon after they began to follow the *Good New Words*.

"What you believe is good, but don't you dare spread it," warned the president.

The council of wise men displayed far less tolerance when the *mayols* ushered in Domingo Hernández Aguilar and Miguel Cashlan, whom they perceived as instigators of this troublesome sect. "Your persistence in speaking against the saints who protect us has put our entire community in danger of epidemic, crop failure, or even worse," maintained the president. "Your neighbors will act justly if they decide to come against you. I cannot protect you. The only means by which you can hope to escape death at the hands of your neighbors during the Carnival is if you stop meeting and stop speaking of this new belief." Secretly, the council had already instructed several *mayols* to purchase bullets and gasoline. They had planned an 'event' later described as a popular uprising of the Chamula people against those who had angered the gods.

Almost in tears, Domingo told Miguel as they left the meeting, *C'usi bal o? Ta persa xcalbe ya'i ti yane!* . . . "What good is it? I have to tell others (the Good News)!"

Forewarned by stool pigeons of the council's plans to have them killed, and fearing the elders might do so that very evening, Miguel

---

[56] **Cargo** — a religious office bestowed as an honor (or a punishment) by the elders of Chamula. The officeholder served at his/her own expense, routinely keeping the officeholder in poverty.

accompanied Domingo back to San Cristóbal where the two spent a restless night in the Jacobs' compound. The next morning, Ken Jacobs accompanied the brothers-in-law to the office of Don Alejandro García, director of the Institute for Indian Affairs (INI) to determine whether some legal steps could be taken to abort the killings.

García was a tough man. He always wore a pistol in a holster strapped to his belt. In addition to his INI post, he was a wealthy man who owned a statewide beer distributorship. He knew the Chamula elders well, both professionally and personally. He had to drive on government roads through their lands to get to property he owned, and was aware of their treachery.

A man of García's demeanor could be counted on to speak frankly. "If the Chamulas say you are dead men, then you are dead men!" laughed the director in a futile effort to diffuse the tense situation.

Miguel smiled. "Don García, there is still God."

García's own smile disappeared. His eyes narrowed as he stated flatly, "There had better be, because you are dead men."

The director dismissed Domingo and Miguel with a promise that he would do whatever he could. At the same time, he advised the men to stay away from the tribe during the Carnival since it would be a drunken brawl and he could offer no protection. "The Chamulas have asked the government never to send soldiers into the tribal lands and we never have," implying he wouldn't send soldiers now, even to protect the marked men. As a result, most believers brought their families into San Cristóbal and stayed in the Jacobs' spacious yard during the four-day festival.

The 1965 Carnival came and went without incident. All believers, with the exception of Miguel and Domingo, returned home. Tribal leaders still had a price on their heads. "The tribe is patient and will not forget their decision to kill us," Domingo brooded. "The only questions are, 'When it will happen? And how it will be done'?"

Although the elders initially meant to kill just the believers' leaders, rumors spread they were now intent on getting rid of every one of the believers. On market days in San Juan Chamula, the president regularly announced over the town square's loudspeaker, "There is no room for these evangelical believers in the tribe. You may deal with them at will." Two believers, previously supplementing their incomes by selling merchandise in the town square, had their booths confiscated. None of the believers were able to meet for worship, for fear of harassment and physical harm. Many were afraid to spend nights in their houses. They worked their fields by day, but slept in the woods or in caves at night. Some stayed with sympathetic neighbors, though no one wanted to be too accommodating, lest they be regarded as Christian and included in the elders' sinister plans.

That same year a flu epidemic pummeled the tribe, and Salvador Me´chij's entire family was hit hard. Salvador mustered his strength and walked for medicine to the only INI clinic in the tribal lands. "There is no medicine available for evangelicals," announced a worker at the clinic, under control of tribal elders. The worker icily suggested Salvador go to Domingo or Miguel for help, then added, "If you turn back from this false teaching, even the shamans will help you."

Salvador somehow walked the long distance to San Cristóbal to seek help from the Jacobs, who sent medicine back with him. By the time he returned, his three-year-old daughter was dead, and his one-year old son died that night. Salvador's neighbors laughed with glee at his loss, taunting, "It must have been the punishment of your God."

As winter gave way to spring, tribal elders found other matters more pressing than harassing the believers. One Sunday, thousands of Chamulas gathered with guns and machetes in the center of San Juan Chamula to protest their heavy tax burden. "Kill them both!" they cried against the tribal president and another tribal elder deemed responsible for the oppressive levy. This was an amazing departure from political protocol, since actions of the elders normally go unquestioned. The popular revolt diverted attention, at least temporarily, from the new believers.

Meanwhile, Domingo, Miguel, and others spent much time in fasting and prayer. "God is the one who knows how to open this tribe to the Gospel," Domingo told the little band of believers, whose numbers had been climbing until the persecution began. With the elders now set against them, those who had expressed interest in the new beliefs were scared off. Even the believers stopped meeting for a while. Then they tried meeting in secret, but Domingo challenged them to meet openly again. "We'll look to God to protect us or let come what He wants to come our way."

Despite continued persecution, the believers kept on telling their countrymen about their new hope. Some conversations took place in San Cristóbal. When traditional healing failed the Chamulas, increasing numbers of people, many of them women, would come to Elaine Jacobs' clinic as a last resort. While receiving medical treatment, the women heard the Gospel from Domingo and Miguel. Later, many bought their husbands to hear these *Good New Words*. The Jacobs' walled yard offered a protected place to learn about the real God, while Ken and Domingo maintained their work on Scripture translation.

To avoid being found together and killed, Miguel and Domingo alternated between staying at their tribal houses and staying in the Jacobs' compound. One evening in October, a well-dressed young Chamula man knocked at the Jacobs' gate. He introduced himself as Xun (*shoon*) and asked if he could speak to Miguel Cashlan. Miguel happened to be in that night. He quietly took the man to the far end of the yard, away from the families awaiting treatment in Elaine's clinic.

"I want to know about the God you worship," began the visitor. "Is it true that He accepts whoever comes to Him, without condition?"

"Yes," declared Miguel. "There are no conditions."

"I ask because I have seen His strength, and I want to know if a deity with that kind of power could truly be good."

Then Xun related his amazing story. "I was one of the many men sent to your house last February to kill you." Miguel's eyes grew wide as Xun continued. "We were a big group. I know we were a big group because before we went to kill you, we drank three large wooden kegs of liquor, and each of us got only a very small amount."

Xun then revealed that when they arrived at Miguel's house, they were prevented by some force from getting close. "A fear came into us that made some of the bravest Chamula men tremble," he said. "We never dared to come any closer, but only looked into the darkness at your house."

The mob decided not to attack Miguel, but to attack his brother-in-law instead. "Again, as we approached Domingo's house, we actually shook with fear," recalled Xun. "Two of our men forced themselves within shouting distance of Domingo's house. When no one replied, they quickly returned to their companions."

Miguel sat wonderfully stunned throughout the story. He clearly remembered after he and Domingo were singled out by the elders for destruction, that they both had spent days fasting and praying. They had asked for God's protection and wondered how they could bring the *Good New Words* to others in the tribe. Now his own assassin was telling him how God's hand had delivered them both. Moreover, the killer wanted to know more about God.

"You, too, can believe," he told Xun.

At this, the young man hung his head. "I would like to enter into the hand of God, like you and Domingo," he said softly, "but my own father would be the first to kill me if I did." Before he left, Xun added these words of warning: "The elders could not kill you earlier this year, but they will try to do it at the end of this month, during *Todos Santos*. Be careful," he urged.

The next Sunday Domingo and Miguel fasted and prayed once again. They praised God for his hand of protection and asked that the *Good New Words* might be sown throughout the tribe by the believers.

ϙ ϙ ϙ ϗ ϙ ϙ ϙ

TODOS SANTOS (Day of the Dead) is celebrated each year from October 31st through November 1st. It corresponds to All Hallows Eve (Halloween) and All Saints Day in Western and European traditions. As a major fiesta in Chamula, *Todos Santos* marks a point at which the physical world is aligned with the spiritual world. Graveyards are cleaned in preparation for the arrival of the spirits of family members recently departed. Everything must be in spiritual harmony, including honoring past traditions. It's a time to cleanse the villages of all impurities, including those worshipping other gods.

In 1965, the festival began on Sunday. This year, Miguel Cashlan would not be cleaning the family graves, marking the path from the

Shamans practice their arts in a former Roman Catholic Church, above, located in the tribal center, San Juan Chamula. Below, a shaman takes the pulse of a child to determine the source of his illness. The boy's father holds a bottle of *pox* (sugar cane liquor) to be used in the diagnostic and healing ceremony. *(Photo of shaman courtesy Tugrul Üke)*

Above, traditional elder Juan Pérez Jolote pronounces words as linguist Ken Jacobs works to learn the language. Below left, Paxcu and her niece Abelina who survived the fiery attack on Paxcu's house. Below right, Domingo Aguilar's son fears his family has been killed by Chamula traditionalists and bursts into tears. *(Photo of Juan Pérez and Ken courtesy of TUGRUL ÜKE)*

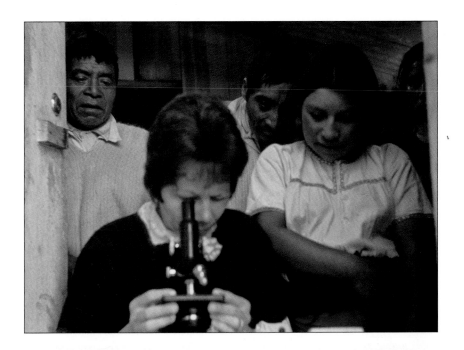

Chamulas crowd around Elaine Jacobs and her microscope, above, claiming her 'magic machine' can tell why a sick person is dying. Below, Domingo Aguilar (left) and Miguel Cashlan in the formal dress of Chamula men, each with a *nuti* slung from one shoulder.

Above, Domingo Aguilar teaches early believers inside the Jacobs' walled compound at San Cristóbal de Las Casas. Down left, Manuel (center) and Tumin Caxtuli (right) accompany the singing of Chamula hymns. Down right, an elder baptizes a new believer in a stream near Mitzitón.

Above left is Mariano Cashlan soon after he began language work with Ken Jacobs. Above right is Tumina, Mariano's wife, weaving a garment in the Jacobs' yard. Below, catechists Javier, Gustavo and Andrés, left to right, insisted on following God's Word and founded the first Chamula church outside the Highlands, in the Lacondon jungle.

The sign above the stage at the November 2001 dedication of the entire Chamula Bible reads: *Now God Also Speaks Chamula*. Down left, a crowd of 10,000 attends the Bible dedication. Down right, Mariano Cashlan looks through the Bible which he and his fellow Chamulas helped to translate.

Above, children of Chamula believers now attend at least some elementary school, like these in Vista Hermosa. Many receive secondary schooling and some attend college. Before the *Good New Words*, most Chamulas provided unskilled labor for the Ladino marketplace. Now, many are skilled laborers or own their own businesses, like the fruit and vegetable vendors in the bottom photo.

Above, evangelist Natil Lorenzo and his wife Juana visit remote Highland villages to share the *Good New Words*. Center, believers worship each Sunday in nearly one hundred churches they have built and paid for themselves. Below, Salvador Patishtán Diaz, who played a key role in translating the OLD TESTAMENT, welcomes Ken and Elaine Jacobs to the church he pastors.

graveyard to the house, and putting out food for the dead—activities he now considered dealing with the devil. Instead he would attend Sunday worship service with other believers.

To avoid giving his enemies an opportunity to strike on a night when zeal for tradition runs high, Miguel attended a worship service at Salvador Me´chij's mother's house, rather than Domingo's house. Besides, Domingo wasn't at his home—he was at the Jacobs' compound in San Cristóbal. Miguel left his wife and one small daughter at home, instructing his wife to build a fire outside on the path to their house and bar the door.

At around 8:30 P.M., she heard the whispers of a large number of men beyond the fire's ring of light. "Miguel must not be home. Let's wait," said the voices.

Miguel's wife countered with her own silent prayer, "Lord, keep them away."

The posse continued their watch until about 11:00 P.M. when Miguel returned alone from the service. Sensing danger as he neared his home, Miguel held his flashlight at arms' length and turned it on. He picked up a large stick and ran toward his house. "In the name of the Lord!" he cried, and the killers fled. Once again, God protected Miguel and his family from the traditionalists who sought to take their lives.

℘ ℘ ℘ ⚕ 𝟿 𝟿 𝟿

As the year waned, it appeared the Chamula believers—especially the believers' leaders—had cheated death, and that the tribal elders might grudgingly accept co-existence. But as Domingo repeatedly pointed out, "They will not forget."

Other murders in a neighboring tribe underscored the simmering conflict across the Chiapan highlands, between traditional religion and evangelical belief. A group of Mitontic[57] believers was ambushed and shot while walking to Sunday services. Two died and three escaped with bullet wounds.

Following those killings, Daniel Aguilar, pastor of the *Church of the Divine Redeemer* in San Cristóbal de Las Casas, led a delegation of two

---

[57] **Mitontic** — one of more than two dozen Tzotzil Mayan tribes. Tribal lands of the Mitontic people border Chamula on the north.

believers from every tribe to the state capitol, where they petitioned the governor to protect the Christians from extermination. The governor sent a deputy to address the elders of each tribe. Despite this intervention, Chamula Christians continued to be told they had better give up their new beliefs before New Year's Day, when the tribes' new civic officers would be installed—or plan to lose their lives. This sent a clear message to everyone: the tribe would maintain the centuries-old customs of its elders and purge any outside religion.

Even so, six Chamula men, their wives and children, and several widows celebrated Christmas together. After attending Christmas Eve services at the *Church of the Divine Redeemer*, the small group prepared and ate a meal together in the Jacobs' yard. They sang SILENT NIGHT and they listened to MATTHEW's account of Jesus' birth—both in the Chamula language.

"Last year, we were only two families," Miguel told everyone, as the celebration wound down about 1:30 A.M. that Christmas morning. "Now we are more, and if the Lord is willing, by next year we will be an even greater number."

One week later, just before New Year's Eve, Miguel's son-in-law approached him with sobering news. The young man told Miguel of a conversation he'd overheard in the back of a *pesero*[58] truck bound for Tsonta Vits.[59] Also on the truck was a large delegation of Chamula leaders carrying big bundles of candles. They were seeking an audience with a *J´ac´chamel*[60]—a killing shaman who performs his deadly rituals in the caves of that mountainous region. Miguel's son-in law heard one of the leaders say, "The deputy from the governor's office put a stop to us killing the Christians with guns and machetes, but there is an even better way to kill all of them."

---

[58] **Pesero** — a van or truck transporting people along a defined route.

[59] **Tsonta Vits** — the well-known center for witchcraft in eastern Chamula.

[60] **J´ac´chamel** — *Giver of Death* (literally).

11
No Looking Back

A LETHAL STORM of tribal vengeance broke with relentless fury on the small band of Chamula Christians early in 1966. Waves of persecution pounded the believers and their leaders with methodical cruelty, threatening to erase the recent gains of this fledgling movement.

Heavily armed mobs fired on both Domingo's and Miguel's homes. Domingo's family survived by pressing their bodies against the dirt floor as bullets ripped over their heads. Warned by a friend, Miguel's family fled into the hills before their killers blocked the trails. Miguel evaded the hit men for six days, then dressed like an old Chamula woman and eventually fled to the safety of the Jacobs' compound in Las Casas. Failing to kill Domingo and Miguel, the tribal authorities turned their attention to the other believers.

THE Sunday afternoon foot traffic in the marketplace at San Juan Chamula had dwindled to a trickle. Manuel and Tumin Caxtuli gathered their merchandise and prepared to close their booth in the open-air market before walking home to Nich'en. Two serious-looking *mayols* approached the brothers. "You need to talk to the president."

"Okay," replied Manuel. "Please let us finish putting away this table and locking up our merchandise." The policemen consented.

This would be the brothers' third meeting with the president.

Several months earlier, Manuel and Tumin had been summoned to appear a second time before the president and the *moletique*. At that meeting, they were warned again to give up their new beliefs and return to the tribal traditions. Just like their first meeting, the brothers said no. Since that first meeting, Manuel and Tumin continued telling relatives, friends, and neighbors about the *Good New Words*. They continued meeting in Manuel's house for study and worship. Other Chamulas from Nich´en and neighboring *parajes*—and from more distant *parajes*—starting attending. Manuel and Tumin tried diligently to follow tradition whenever possible, to show the elders they were not challenging all tribal beliefs—only those with respect to religion.

As the brothers put their table and merchandise into storage, they remembered what Jesus told his disciples to do when they were handed over to the local authorities.[61] The Caxtulis knelt privately in their tiny storage room. "Lord, we don't know what to do or say," confessed Manuel. "We've answered as honestly as we could. These are our elders and we need to respect them, but we can't turn our backs on you. Please give us the words to speak to the president and the tribal authorities." The brothers locked the door and walked with the policemen to the office of the president.

The elders sat while Domingo Lunes, now in his second year as president of Chamula, stood and explained his summons. "We've told you twice to stop speaking about these *New Words* and the foreign god who said them, but you continue to speak and force others to believe."

"We're not forcing anybody to believe," replied Tumin. "When people come and ask, we tell them what we believe. They come willingly. Why can't we tell them?"

"Because you are not perpetuating the traditions we've received from our parents and grandparents through centuries of belief," said the president. All the elders nodded their assent. "Give up what you are believing and go back, or you will wish you had," demanded Domingo Lunes.

"We can't stop believing now," said Manuel. "We've believed for too

---

[61] MARK 13:9–11/NIV: "...You will be handed over to the local councils and flogged in the synagogues. On account of Me you will stand before governors and kings as witnesses to them. And the Gospel must first be preached to all nations. Whenever you are arrested and brought to trial, do not worry beforehand about what to say. Just say whatever is given to you at the time, for it is not you speaking, but the Holy Spirit."

long and this is something we're convinced is from the true creator, God."

"Then we'll have to put you in jail," the president threatened.

Another elder added, "Jail's a scary place. Sometimes people get hurt in jail. They get beaten or killed. Aren't you afraid of jail?"

"I'll have to accept that," said Manuel, trying to be respectful, yet determined to stand his ground. "You are the responsible people—the tribal authorities. If you send me to jail, I must go; but remember this, I haven't done anything wrong."

At 3:00 P.M. that afternoon, the *moletique* adjourned. They had decided to let Tumin go, perhaps to carry a warning to the others. But the *mayols* escorted Manuel to the jail in the rear of the *cabildo* at San Juan Chamula.

Iron bars formed the outside wall of the jail cells. This allowed families to feed the prisoners—and enabled the public to taunt them. To his surprise Manuel found two familiar faces already behind bars—his father, Sebastián Caxtuli,[62] and Salvador Me'chij. The authorities had clamped down on not just Manuel, but on a trio of 'believers.'

Later that evening tribal officials transported the trio to San Cristóbal de Las Casas, where they were thrown into the city jail for drunks. The following morning, Manuel, Sebastián, and Salvador were brought before a local Ladino judge. The prisoners saw other familiar faces in the courtroom: Ken Jacobs and Garold Van Engen (Garold, also from the United States, was working with the Presbyterian Church of Mexico).

Also present were the men's accusers, Domingo Lunes and other tribal officials who charged the three men with plotting to kill the president. "That's not true," declared Manuel, when he heard these charges. "We read the Bible and there is no place in the Bible where Jesus teaches us to kill people who are persecuting us." The judge motioned for him to continue. "This all started about a year ago when they told me not to believe any more."

Domingo Lunes interrupted. "I know you're the ones who want to kill me, and that is why we don't want you in Chamula. If you want to believe this Bible, that's up to you, but we don't want you living in our villages."

---

[62] Sebastián had not yet professed belief, but was jailed because of his association with the believers in his family.

At that point the judge spoke up. "So this is really not about a murder plot; it's about religion. Article twenty-four of the Constitution guarantees these men the freedom to believe whatever they want. If this is not about killing, then there is no reason for them to be in jail. Set them free."

﹥ ﹥ ﹥ ✄ ﹤ ﹤ ﹤

KEN and Garold relocated Manuel, Sebastián, and Salvador to the Jacobs' spacious yard. There the trio continued to witness the scope of persecution descending upon the new Christians. In addition to seeing their own families, they encountered nearly every Chamula who had openly declared themselves followers of the *Good New Words*. They had all fled the tribal highlands and taken refuge in the Las Casas yard surrounded by protective walls. As word spread that Manuel and the others had been arrested, the new believers—now numbering almost forty—fled Chamula territory. They left behind homes, cornfields, chickens and turkeys, and all their meager earthly possessions.

Ken and Elaine provided blankets and whatever sleeping space they could find. Three men slept in the Jacobs' luggage trailer, one family bedded down atop a pile of corn, and three girls accepted the wheat bin as their room. Others made do elsewhere in the compound.

Early the next morning Manuel, Sebastián, and several others quietly made their way back into the highlands. What they found confirmed their worst fears. Someone had tried burning down both Miguel's and Domingo's houses by igniting kerosene splattered against the door jams. Although both homes suffered only minor damage, the doors of the Caxtulis' homes had been ripped off the hinges, and their furnishings slashed by machetes. Barking dogs soon warned that someone else was approaching. Quickly the refugees gathered a few possessions and once again, fled for the hills.

Around sunrise the next morning, the cold, tired, hungry band returned to Las Casas. Sebastián, father of the Caxtuli brothers, dragged himself through the gate. Sebastián suffered from tuberculosis and was coughing violently. He plopped down next to his tiny sack of corn—the only thing he'd salvaged the night before. His labored breathing was heavy as he coughed up blood.

Elaine fixed hot coffee and toast for the women, while the men built fires to warm themselves in the early morning chill. Ken suggested singing HE'S COMING SOON, a chorus which he had recently translated with Domingo's help. "Brother Canuto," asked Sebastián, recovering from his coughing spell. "Is Jesus really coming soon?"

Yes," replied Ken. "The *Good New Words* say He's coming in the same way he left—in the clouds."

Considering this for a moment, Sebastián replied, "Brother, I sure hope he comes before my bag of corn runs out."

❧ ❧ ❧ ❧ ❧ ❧ ❧

THE material loss was devastating. They'd given up nearly everything. But no one said they'd give up following Christ. Initially none of the believers returned permanently to their tribal areas for fear they'd be ambushed on the trails or murdered in their houses. Other family members quietly kept the believers posted. Enemies were watching the trails and boasting, "Before long, not a single Christian will be alive." Mexican authorities, though sympathetic, seemed helpless to stop the wild mob action encouraged behind the scenes by the elders.

Unable to go home and dependent on the kindness of outsiders, the Chamula believers, young in their faith, began to realize they were not alone in their battle. Christians near and far came to their aid. A visiting veterinarian offered to replace six sheep rather than see a young woman risk a night journey back into the highlands to fetch her only source of wool for weaving. A San Diego businessman expressed intention to raise money for home reconstruction. Believers from a neighboring tribe provided sacks of corn for tortillas. Some of the Jacobs' supporters provided money for food.

Having experienced similar persecution, a neighboring Huisteco elder named Nicholas spoke with the Chamula believers. "Our Savior Himself tells us we are blessed when people persecute us and say all kinds of evil against us for His sake," noted Nicholas, speaking from

MATTHEW 5:11–12. "When this happens, we are to rejoice, for our reward in heaven will be great."

Hearing this greatly encouraged several of the exiled Chamulas. That night Domingo led the congregation in this prayer: "If not for You, oh Lord, we wouldn't call each other brothers (referring to the Huistecos), but now we do. Thank You for loving us and thank You that even Ken and Elaine's friends have mercy on us." The small, fire-tested Chamula church began to understand they were part of a wider community of believers.

The displaced believers now faced new challenges as they tried living together in a confined area. Everyone knew everyone else's business. The lack of firewood sometimes sparked terse exchanges. But the close quarters also aided the translation effort. Since the Chamulas were now worshipping on his property, Ken could see first-hand his translations being used, and judge his effort's accuracy from discussions they generated. The young church met three times each week and on special occasions. Before each service, Ken would teach Domingo the Scripture they'd be using, and Domingo would explain it to the church as he led them in worship. By this time Ken and Domingo had also completed FIRST and SECOND THESSALONIANS, several OLD TESTAMENT stories, and sixteen hymns in the Chamula language. Now they were working on the BOOK OF ACTS.

The Chamula believers were showing signs of growing in spiritual wisdom. Each Sunday the young church fasted and prayed that the Lord would permit them to return to their homes and that His Word would be received among all Chamulas. While they longed to be back in the tribe, their leaders continually reminded them, "We're not true believers if we only tell God what we want Him to do for us and fail to be willing to do whatever He asks of us."

As spring approached, the Mexican authorities arranged a shaky truce with tribal authorities to allow believers back into the highlands. However, the truce offered no guarantee of safety. Rumors circulated that tribal elders had organized gangs in each of the tribal sectors to harass Christians. As a result, no one spent the night back in the tribe, but they were able to plant their fields during daylight hours. For the next sixteen months most believers spent part of their days within the tribe, but returned to sleep in the Jacobs' compound at night. During this time their numbers grew steadily, aided by a ballooning notoriety. Not all tribal members had turned against them and some were curious about a belief so powerful that a fellow Chamula would risk everything to possess it.

After being jailed, Manuel Caxtuli assumed no one else would want to hear the *Good New Words*. But the opposite was true. "Everybody who heard I had been jailed came and asked what I was jailed for. I told them I was jailed for believing in God, and they asked, 'What did you believe about God?' and 'What is different from the way we believe'?" Since other Chamulas kept asking him all these questions, Manuel no longer needed to look for opportunities to share his faith. The opportunities came to him—constantly. Many of those inquisitive Chamulas were from several villages where the *Good New Words* had not been heard. Domingo, Miguel, Manuel, and others began traveling to these villages. They'd visit new believers wherever they could find them, and teach others who expressed interest in the *Good New Words*. At the same time, other Chamulas—whom the Jacobs had never met—began showing up in their Las Casas yard, asking to buy a copy of the GOSPEL OF MARK or to speak to one of the believers. The Gospel made inroads even among some shamans, who in Chamula tradition are indispensable 'intercessors' between the physical tribe and the spirit world.

AN old shaman living near Domingo's house in the tribal territory became terribly sick. She had already spent more than three hundred pesos on *curanderos*[63] and instead of improving, she grew steadily worse. Rumor had it her *chanul* (companion animal) was a coyote that attacked some sheep and left unfinished carcasses lying in the hills. The owner of the sheep placed poison on one of the carcasses. When the unwitting coyote returned, he ate some of the poisoned meat. Thus, what was happening to the coyote was reflected in the old woman's body.

Domingo was back in the tribal territory at the time. Since the sick

---

[63] **Curandero** — Spanish for *healer*, another local name used for the healing shamans. In the mid 1960s, 300 pesos was worth about $24 U.S. dollars.

woman had no bath house, Domingo let her know that she could use his. Afterward he invited her in for coffee. He explained the *Good New Words* and the claim of Christ on her life. "I used to believe in the spirits, but now I trust in Christ," said Domingo. He encouraged her to do the same, then prayed for her, and for the first time in weeks the old woman was able to eat. During the next few days he provided medicines and finally guided her to the Jacobs' compound. Now under Elaine's tender care, the old woman underwent a week of intravenous injections for a liver infection. The former shaman returned to her home in Chamula feeling like a new woman—insisting that she wanted, with all her heart, to follow Christ.

Another shaman from Tsonta Vits[64] brought his daughter to Las Casas. Again, Elaine was able to successfully treat another life-threatening illness. That experience also brought this shaman to the Lord.[65]

News of these healings and conversions of both shamans spread throughout the highlands like flames fanned by wind. The traditional elders realized, that in spite of their threats, these followers of Jesus remained effective in winning others. Consequently the tribal authorities redoubled their efforts against the leadership of the Chamula church, particularly Domingo and Miguel. The fencing around Domingo's fields was cut to pieces. Two of Miguel's neighbors were hired by the elders to watch for opportunities to overpower him. Warned by friends, Miguel confronted both men. One trembled with fear as he admitted his intent; he even gave details of a previous attempt to burn both Domingo's and Miguel's houses. Miguel took pains to explain to both his neighbors that he forgave them, and the two were so moved that they agreed to consider the claims of the *Good New Words*.

As 1967 dawned, the Jacobs began construction on a new medical clinic building (they'd been using rooms in their own home) and new guest facilities. The new guest facilities could accommodate leaders of house churches throughout the tribe who wanted to study Scriptures one day a week. It was Domingo's idea that such leaders could take the lessons they would learn back to their own villages and teach others

---

[64] **Tsonta Vits** — the well-known center for witchcraft in eastern Chamula.

[65] The conversions of Chamula shamans were significant. In the neighboring tribe of Huistan, which Christianity had penetrated eight years earlier, there was not yet a shaman who had become a believer.

who wanted to believe.

By this time, most of the initial group of forty believers remained inside the adobe-walled sanctuary of the Jacob's compound. They traveled back to the tribe only to work their fields, and then only during daylight hours. Several of their tribal friends and neighbors were now expressing interest in the *Good New Words*. Despite being taunted frequently by hecklers, and hearing threats against their leaders, none of the believers had been killed. But that was about to change.

ᒉ ᒉ ᒉ ⳾ ᒋ ᒋ ᒋ

ON August 23, 1967, Ken and Elaine Jacobs, on temporary assignment with SIL at the University of North Dakota, received the following telegram from another missionary colleague, Chuck Bennett:[66]

ONE HOUSE BURNED EASTERN GROUP CHAMULA AUGUST 18. THREE CHILDREN DEAD. TWO HOSPITALIZED. OTHERS THREATENED NIGHTLY. ALL, INCLUDING DOMINGO, VERY FRIGHTENED. YOUR PRESENCE NEEDED IF POSSIBLE.

Launching a volley of violence against members of the young church, Chamula traditionalists ramped up their loathsome efforts to rid the tribe of Christians. In addition to Xalic's fiery, murderous attack on eighteen-year-old Paxcu, reported by telegram to Ken and Elaine, mobs encircled other believers' homes and taunted their families.

Threats on their leaders' lives skyrocketed. One night soon after the attack on Paxcu's home, tribal leaders made good on two years' worth of threats. Domingo was staying in the Jacobs' compound while Ken and Elaine were in the United States. Miguel's family was staying in Domingo's tribal home, which still housed Domingo's wife and their five children; about fourteen people bedded down there that night.

In the darkness the house was surrounded by 200 or more armed Chamula men. When Miguel became aware of their dire situation, he yelled, "Throw yourselves on the floor and call on the Lord!" Suddenly the inside of the roof burst into flames. Just like they'd done to Paxcu's house, the mob had splashed gasoline through openings in the eaves,

---

[66] At the time Chuck Bennett was a pilot with Mission Aviation Fellowship. He later became MAF's president.

ignited it, and now stood by ready to gun down anyone fleeing the burning building. But the flames quickly petered out. So they sloshed more gasoline onto the smoking thatch. For a second time the flames—somehow—miraculously disappeared.

When the house failed to ignite, the angry rabble spent the next two hours firing their guns into the house. Throughout this entire onslaught, only Miguel's eight-year-old daughter, Rafaela, was hurt.

Rafaela had raised her head as bullets ricocheted within the one-room adobe house. One bullet tore through her cheek, slicing out an upper tooth. "I'm hit! I'm dying, Papa!" she cried. Miguel crawled to his daughter's side. She spit both the bullet and the tooth into his hand. After this two-hour, multi-gun deluge, the killers tried to break down the door with the butts of their guns, but the door held tight.

The Chamula believers living within the tribal region realized they were all ripe for this kind of violence. During the next two weeks, the believers slept in the woods and rocky hills surrounding their homes. Understandably, they grew more fearful of simply carrying out their ordinary daytime activities without being attacked. Deciding that protecting their lives was more important than protecting their pigs, chickens, and sheep, or their yet-to-be-harvested crops, they abandoned their homes en mass. Within days the Chamula believers descended into the Jacobs' walled yard in Las Casas—the second such mass relocation many of these people had experienced in two years. Again this time, most arrived with nothing except the clothes they were wearing.

This exodus was more difficult for the Chamula believers than the first exodus. This time they left behind ripe crops in the field; and the number of believers had more than doubled. The first time around they were less than forty—but God had heard their prayers and answered: now they numbered more than one hundred![67] With help from the believers' leadership, the Jacobs erected a temporary cooking shelter. But they all soon realized the generously sized yard was not generous enough to support this large number of refugees for long.

Domingo and Ken tried to rent housing in Las Casas for the dis-

---

[67] Chamula believers exceeded one hundred despite five families returning to the tribal religion because they considered the cost of following Christ too great.

placed families. Even as a handful of houses were located, questions remained. How would more than one hundred people driven from their homes and land support themselves for the next few months? What would they do if the tribe decided never to allow them to set foot in Chamula again? What would they eat? What would happen to their unharvested crops? To whom could they appeal for redress of grievances? As the rainy season ended and the cold season set in, these questions tumbled through the minds of the displaced believers.

Soon after their tribal exodus the Chamula church met for worship. Despite meeting behind the safety of the Jacobs' walled yard, they shifted their meeting time to Saturday night. Saturday evening offered fewer tribal members in Las Casas who might report on them. During this worship service, the believers prayed about their persecution—and for their persecutors. They studied passages from GENESIS concerning Abraham's wealthy nephew Lot who lost his home and all other earthly possessions when urged to flee with his family to the hills—as fire rained down on Sodom and Gomorrah. But Lot's wife still longed for Sodom. Although warned not to, she looked back and instantly became a pillar of salt.[68] The comparison between that OLD TESTAMENT family and their own dire circumstances became the theme of their worship that chilly November evening in 1967.

The believers encouraged each other to hold fast to the promises of the *Good New Words*. "Let us not be like Lot's wife and not be willing to leave our lands, houses, crops and animals for Jesus' sake."

12
Taking God Seriously

THE TWENTY-TWO Chamula families who fled to Ken and Elaine Jacobs' yard in the fall of 1967 would encounter yet more adversity. Homeless and living as nomads, they'd been forced into a Ladino world that had never recognized them as equals and now barely tolerated their presence. Nor did the Mexican government offer them much hope of returning to the land of their birth.

Early in 1968, four leaders of the young church traveled to Mexico City to appeal for national intervention. They succeeded in gaining an audience with Mexico's Vice-President who presented them with a signed document declaring their religious freedom. But how would they communicate this to tribal elders, let alone (at the time) 40,000 tribal members? Many of their fellow Chamulas still thought all Christians should be killed, and Mexican police were unwilling to challenge the authority of the elders on tribal land.

Jealousies, resentments, and petty quarrels began straining this congregation of homesick Christians packed into close quarters. They struggled—just like many people struggle—to apply their faith to their present circumstances. Willpower alone was not sufficient; even their leadership was in flux. Ken released his language helper, Domingo Hernández Aguilar, after he abandoned his common-law wife to marry another woman. Shunned by the other believers, Domingo departed—leaving a leadership void behind.

As winter turned to spring, Miguel Cashlan and the Caxtuli brothers provided important help to the other believers. They rented land on the outskirts of San Cristóbal for each family to grow their corn, beans, and squash. But no one else seemed as uniquely equipped as Domingo had been to assist with the spiritual needs of the fledgling congregation. New assistance, coupled with a boost to the translation efforts, would come from an unlikely source.

PERCHED on a three-legged stool amid a dozen hens pecking at the kernels of grain he'd just scattered on the ground, Mariano Gómez Hernández—better known as Mariano Cashlan—gazed intently at the book lying open in his lap. Born in the Chamula village of Ya´al Vacax, Mariano spent much of his early life away from home. As a youngster he followed his father, Miguel Cashlan, to the coffee plantations. By age sixteen he'd already put in six years of work on the *fincas*.[69]

For the next few years Mariano lived on his own, both in and out of Chamula territory. Recently married, he and his wife Tumina had been staying with his family in Ya´al Vacax, despite a strained relationship with his father. The young couple found themselves homeless when tribal elders drove Christians and their families from their homes. Not yet believers themselves, Mariano and Tumina had no personal resources; eventually they took refuge with other family members in the Jacobs' compound.[70] Though the yard was already overflowing with people, Ken and Elaine made room for them in a converted chicken coop. They slept in a tiny feed room separated from the chickens by a thin wooden door. After feeding the chickens that July morning in 1968, Mariano stared at the first page of the book he'd been given.

Mariano had learned to read and write some Spanish during his years in the *fincas*. But the book on his lap was printed in the Chamula language. Until this morning he'd never seen his tribal language in print. He sounded out some of the words, since Ken had organized Chamula letters and their sounds in a manner similar to their Spanish counterparts. After struggling through the first few lines of print, Mariano was delighted to discover he understood what the writer of the book, a man named MARK, was saying. He kept reading.

---

[69] **Hugh Steven** (1976), *They Dared to Be Different* (Eugene OR: Harvest House Publishers), p. 32.

[70] *Ibid.*, pp. 94–95, 108.

A few pages into the book, the words of a man called Jesus abruptly confronted Mariano. He had been told by his uncle that Jesus was the Son of the Living God. "Your father Miguel and I have both placed our trust in this God," Domingo had said. "You would do well to consider believing, too." Mariano was somewhat intrigued. He'd seen a dramatic change in his father's life; Miguel no longer got drunk and beat his wife. Still, the young man was skeptical of this new faceless Deity, having been raised to worship the colorfully clothed statues of saints in the church at San Juan Chamula. He did, however, accept Domingo's gift of the book he was now reading, along with a small book of hymns, also in the Chamula language.

The English equivalent of the Chamula words Mariano read that summer morning were:

IF THERE IS SOMETHING EVIL THAT YOUR HEART WANTS TO DO AND YOU START TO BRING TO FRUITION THAT SIN BY MEANS OF YOUR HAND, STOP! DON'T DO IT! TREAT YOURSELF AS THOUGH YOU HAVE CUT OFF YOUR HAND. BETTER TO DO THAT AND GO INTO THE HAND OF GOD, THAN TO GO INTO THE FIRE THAT NEVER GOES OUT![71]

Mariano was familiar with the Maya belief in a lower world populated by bad spirits. The Christians called that fiery world hell.

Preoccupied by images these words created, Mariano stopped reading and stared through the woven wire of the chicken coop. He was a deeply troubled man, haunted and imprisoned by bad choices he continued to make. He hated his father for verbally and physically abusing him as a child. His father had obviously changed with his conversion to Christianity, but a huge chasm still remained. Raised in an animistic culture, Mariano dreaded—and stood in awe of—the shamans with the power to heal and to destroy. He feared the elders who threatened to kill anyone refusing to obey Chamula law. He also hated the Ladinos because they had the power and possessions he craved.[72] Because he spent so much of his life among the outsiders, his fellow Chamulas considered Mariano a *cashlan*, just like his father. Most of all, Mariano hated his own shortcomings. He had failed to win the love of his father.

---

[71] MARK 2:44–45

[72] **Hugh Steven** (1976), *They Dared to Be Different* (Eugene OR: Harvest House Publishers), pp. 32–33.

He had failed to appease the Chamula gods of wood and stone. Now, as he searched for peace in what Domingo called the *Good New Words*, he came face to face with a strange new Deity, an invisible Greatness who also required perfection. Based on his past failures, Mariano knew he could never measure up. "My uncle's God is no different from the countless gods worshiped by our ancestors," thought Mariano, as he reread the words in MARK about the consequences of uncurbed evil.

Then his thoughts reverted to the tribal elders' teachings: "Fall near a spring and lose your soul. Make a wrong move and you are doomed." As a child, Mariano became ill after tripping and falling next to a spring where a water god was said to reside. The attending shaman told Mariano's mother that the spirit of the spring had seized her son's soul and would not let go without a sacrificial substitute. His mother purchased a chicken which the shaman killed in Mariano's presence so the spirit would release the boy's soul in exchange for the spirit of the fowl.[73]

"Like the gods I've been running from all my life, the Father of this Jesus expects perfection from his followers," concluded Mariano. He reflected on his own casually wicked life of envy and hate, drunkenness, dispute, and sexual conquest, and as he did, he felt cornered by the words he was reading. Squirming on the low stool he tried to shift the blame to this new God—if he really did exist. "Who do you think you are, making me the way I am?" he said, accusing God of creating his voracious appetite for sin. "You know what I am like, and now you put restrictions on me." At first, Mariano thought he had a good argument, but he didn't have the last word. Every time he reviewed those few words of Jesus in his own language, he could not escape the fact that if he failed to deal with his sins, the fire of hell would be his destiny.

Cold fear gripped his heart. Mariano closed the book. "Is there no other way?" he asked. For a brief time he considered returning to the Chamula religious structure as an antidote for his inner turmoil. But in his heart Mariano knew this repressive system of ritual drunkenness and animal sacrifice could never offer the peace for which his soul now yearned.

He picked up the little Chamula hymnbook. Leafing through, he came to a section in the back entitled the TEN COMMANDMENTS. "So this is

[73] *Ibid.*, pp. 30–32.

what I need to obey to gain eternal life," Mariano mused. He read as far as the SEVENTH COMMANDMENT: "You shall not commit adultery." A familiar wave of guilt and hopelessness washed over him. The more he read, the more troubled he grew. "This is not medicine for my soul, but rather chains that bind my uncooperative body," he lamented with disgust.

Mariano threw down the hymnbook and stormed out of the coop. Leaving the Jacobs' walled yard by the side door, he walked to the outskirts of San Cristóbal de Las Casas. Alone under the majestic highland pine trees, he bowed down and spoke once again to the invisible Greatness he'd encountered in the *Good New Words*, but this time with an open soul. "Oh, God!" groaned Mariano. "I am a man without hope, unless you have a better way."

DOMINGO had departed the Jacobs' compound in early 1968. Half a year later, Ken still had not found someone else to replace Domingo as his language helper. The translation effort nearly ground to a halt by the time the young couple Mariano and Tumina arrived. Elaine watched that first day as Mariano played with her son, Jerry, tossing the boy in the air and catching him in strong arms. In the next few days she noticed Mariano answering almost every question eagerly and intelligently, and that he had learned to read his native Chamula language with exceptional speed. "Why don't you try out Mariano as a language helper?" she proposed to Ken. Ken asked. Mariano agreed to try it out, and impressed his employer by reporting for his first day of work wearing a beautiful white *chamarro*.[74]

Mariano loved translation and excelled at it. From his first day on the job, the young man demonstrated his unique gift for transferring ideas from one language to another, maintaining both fidelity and intelligibility. Seated hours at a time at Ken's translation desk, Mariano remained conscientious and alert throughout their sessions. Day after day, month after month, the two made steady progress on the Chamula NEW TESTAMENT. They completed first drafts of the ACTS OF THE APOSTLES, the GOSPEL OF LUKE, PAUL'S LETTER TO THE ROMANS, and the *Good New Words* according to MATTHEW. Then one day it happened.

---

[74] The equivalent of a suit in Western culture.

They'd begun work on the BOOK OF HEBREWS. That afternoon, while putting the finishing touches on Chapters Eight through Ten, Mariano abruptly stopped his work. The passage talked about the blood of bulls and goats sacrificed annually on the altar, and that these sacrifices were only a shadow of the one perfect sacrifice Jesus made for all time and for all sins on the cross. Mariano was familiar with sacrifices. His Maya ancestors tried to appease the gods' anger with the blood of sinful humans. "I can hardly believe that what I'm hearing in the *Good New Words* is true," he said with astonishment.

"Tell me, Mariano, what are you hearing that is so hard to believe?" prodded Ken, willing to take an occasional detour with this bright, hard-working language assistant.

Mariano paused, searching for words to convey his thoughts. "If my understanding of what we are translating is correct, the *Good New Words* are not an *order*, but an *offer* made to all the people of the world," said the Chamula man, who until this moment had only known gods which made demands on their subjects.

"What is the offer?" asked Ken.

With his employer's indulgence, Mariano began describing what he had gleaned from the Scriptures he'd been helping translate—how this God sent his Son to earth to live a perfect life and to die on the cross with the weight of all the sins ever committed, or ever to be committed, on his shoulders. This Jesus was buried, and after three days he was raised from the dead. He appeared to many people and was later taken to heaven, where he now sits at the right hand of his Father and speaks on behalf of his followers.

"If I understand correctly," summarized Mariano, "the sins of all the people in the world that have kept them from God are forgiven. Jesus' sacrifice has wiped them all away. Because of this, I'm hearing that any man, no matter who he is, may get up and go to God, Who sees him well. No one will stop him, not even God himself."

Ken wisely concealed the smile growing inside his own heart.

"That's not all," said Mariano, recalling how guilty and hopeless he felt, realizing he could never live the TEN COMMANDMENTS. "In the BOOK OF HEBREWS, I'm hearing that a man may act like he's a good person but that it is impossible for him to meet God's standards," he said. "There is really no point in trying."

"I am also hearing that, because of Jesus' sacrifice, God stands before us and points to Himself, saying, 'Look, I make Myself responsible to do for you what you cannot do for yourself'," said the young Chamula. "By writing His laws in our minds and on our hearts, and by sending the Spirit of Jesus to be our Helper, God promises to govern our lives and help us live a life that is pleasing to Him—to take us from where we are to where He wants us to go." Mariano fell silent, lost in his thoughts. Was this really the answer to his plea, months ago under the highland pines?

"If that is God's offer and you wanted to accept it, what would you say to Him?" asked Ken.

Mariano thought for a moment, then declared, "I would take seriously and hold in high esteem what God had obligated Himself to do." In that brief exchange, the translator and his language helper discovered the Chamula expression for faith.

Mariano did not take the step right away. In his heart he understood what it would cost to accept God's better way. No longer would Mariano be the responsible party in his life, but he would let God's Spirit take over and reside in him. He didn't understand exactly how that would work, but Mariano knew instinctively that he would no longer be in charge. Still, it was hard to give up control—even after failing repeatedly to manage his own affairs.

One morning just a few days later, Mariano arrived at the translation desk and told Ken, "That's what I want!" His heart now at peace, the language helper and the translator worked together from that point on as true brothers in Christ. Their new, growing relationship helped further enhance the quality of their work. Mariano later remarked to Ken, "When I heard and understood the *Good New Words* as an *offer* instead of an order, everything you and I were translating began to make sense."

13
Lose My Sin In Your Heart

MARIANO'S SEARCH had ended. In welcoming God's better way, he came to appreciate what St. Paul wrote to the believers in Rome almost 2,000 years earlier: "Therefore, since we have been justified by faith, we have peace with God through our Lord Jesus Christ."[75] The English rendition of Mariano and Ken's translation into Chamula would read, "In view of the fact that we are seen well by God because we have taken His offer seriously, we are one-hearted with God because of our Lord Jesus Christ."

God had not been at war with Mariano; Mariano had been at war with God. By taking seriously what God had obligated Himself to do, Mariano's conflict had ended. Mariano began a new life of peace, or as the Chamulas would say, "being one-hearted with God."

A new chapter had also begun in the story of God delivering His Word to this particular Maya people in their mother tongue. The Chamula language had few words for abstracts like *faith*, so Ken and Mariano were constantly searching for phrases to convey the meaning of these important concepts. Because his role in translation had intersected his quest for forgiveness and acceptance, Mariano unexpectedly discovered faith. At last he was qualified to express this concept in the Chamula language. Together, now as partakers of the same Spirit, the two men devoted themselves to finding the right idioms to correctly communicate other abstracts crucial to understanding God's offer:

Repentance — The Chamulas use two reflexive verbs to com-

[75] ROMANS 5:1/NIV.

municate the biblical concept of repentance. *Xca'i jba* means *to know* or *to reflect inwardly on one's self*. This self inquiry or self examination is similar to the attitude of the prodigal son where LUKE 15:17 records that "he came to his senses." Broke, starving, and slopping hogs, the prodigal admitted to himself that he was in the wrong place. The second reflexive verb *jsutes jba* means *turning away from what one is and turning to something else*. In a sense, it is deciding against one's self and toward someone else. It is similar to the attitude of the prodigal son when he said, "I will get up and go to my father" (v. 18).

 Forgiveness — Any sin or wrongdoing that is forgiven either by God or by man is *ch'aybil xa*, meaning *it has been lost*. Since the Chamula language contains no ability to say, "Will you forgive my sin?", the mode of expression is *ch'aybun ti jmule* which translates to *lose for me my sin!*

Justification — The sin-cleansed status a person is given by God, when that person accepts by faith the reconciling work of God through Jesus Christ, is referred to in the Scriptures as justification (declared righteous). The Chamulas use two different ways to express this concept. One of those is *Lec xij'ilatotic yu'un Dios ta sventa ti ta xc'ot ta o'ntonal ta xch'unel ti Jesucristoe*. The English equivalent would read, *We are seen well by God because of our faith in Jesus Christ*.

These rich verbal phrases, constructed to convey abstracts and figures of speech to the Chamulas, also enhanced Ken's understanding of Scriptures he had taken for granted since his youth. For example, PSALM 119:130/NIV states, "The unfolding of Your words gives light: it gives understanding to the simple." *The unfolding* was a figure of speech which meant nothing to the Chamulas. Rendered in English, the Chamula restatement of this verse reads: "When God's Word is clarified, it gives you information so that even the person who is unschooled can make decisions that will benefit him."

Frequently the way Chamulas restated Scriptures to make them understandable in their culture had the effect of clarifying Ken's own concept of God. Ken acknowledged, "The Chamulas told us what they were hearing in the *Good New Words*; we never told them. These uniquely Chamula statements, rendered in English, became to me like mentors. They would define God to me, and Mariano was my teacher."

ℰ ℰ ℰ ✄ ? ? ?

As Mariano learned to live life under the government of God, the process of transferring Biblical concepts into the *Chamula Tzotzil* language left a deep, lasting impression on both the translator and his language helper. Another concept was *love*.

Love and respect between Chamula couples, or rather the lack of it, has often been illustrated by this well-worn Mexican joke:

An Indian man and his wife were returning from a distant market. A Mexican man meeting them on the trail noticed the Indian man carrying only a machete, and a lady trudging far behind him with a crying baby hanging from her neck and an oversized load on her back. "Is that your wife following you?" asked the Mexican. "Yes," replied the Indian, gruffly. "Then, why is she carrying that big load?" asked the Mexican. Astonished he would even ask such a question, the Indian man replied, "Because it's heavy!"

A young Chamula man like Mariano had no example or moral foundation on which to build a relationally healthy married life. If he followed tribal standards, he would never speak to the woman he intended to take. He would simply say, "I want her! I will negotiate with her parents for her. I will pay the bride price. She will be mine!" As time went by, he would think of her as his property and treat her accordingly.

Young Chamula women, growing into marriageable maturity beginning at age twelve, were seldom free from the lustful eyes of young Chamula men appraising potential brides. The bashful girls hid their youthful giggles behind protective shawls, enjoying the obvious attention they attracted. But this temporary pleasure was overshadowed by horror stories of mistreatment from their husbands, as told by older women who advised their daughters and nieces, "Never get married!"

One day Ken and Mariano found themselves translating EPHESIANS 5:22–33, which talks about God's standards for the husband-wife relationship. Mariano had subverted the traditional way of obtaining a wife by convincing Tumina to elope, but like other Chamula men, he regularly put her interests behind his and demeaned her publicly when it suited his purposes. He did not even address her by name. *Ants!*... "Woman!" he would say. This was not always used in a derogatory manner, but neither did it reflect tenderness.

As the translator and his helper began work on the passage in EPHESIANS, neither had any thought of how translating the concept "husbands love your wives" would affect Mariano. After considerable discussion, Mariano settled on an equivalent phrase: *Viniquetic, ac´o ti lec oy ti avajnil ta aventa!*... "Husbands, be sure your wives are the beneficiaries of who you are and what you do!"

After uttering these words Mariano remained silent for a long time. What the *Good New Words* seemed to be telling Chamula husbands now became a personal message to Mariano. Tumina was not to be treated with contempt or disgrace. Rather, he should elevate his wife and do things for *her* gain, rather than *his* gain. She was to be his beneficiary; he was to be her benefactor. His model was Jesus who gave Himself up for everyone in the world, including Mariano.

When Ken attempted to break the silence, Maranio interrupted. "My marriage is all wrong," he said. "Tumina is not the beneficiary of who I am and what I do; I have her for my benefit." Before Ken could comment on this unexpected outburst, Mariano spoke again. "Canuto, what must I do?" For a long moment Ken sat in silence, wondering how to answer. But Ken didn't need to reply, since the younger man answered his own inquiry. Getting up from the translation desk, Mariano said, "I know what I must do. He walked across the yard to the small brick house where he and Tumina now lived.

Months before, Mariano had committed adultery with a young girl who lived in the Jacobs' yard, and Tumina had caught them in the act. Though he had confessed to God and to Ken, Mariano had not asked forgiveness of Tumina. "Besides," he reasoned in his heart, "I would not have looked beyond our house had she not withheld herself from me." But what Mariano had discovered in the *Good New Words* had changed his heart.

He walked into the house where Tumina was making tortillas for their evening meal. "Tumina," began Mariano, addressing her by name for the first time in weeks. "I have sinned against you." He related what she already knew about his adultery and his unwillingness to accept this sexual indiscretion as his own fault. "Most important of all, I have not put your interests ahead of mine since the day we were married," he confessed. "Will you lose my sin in your heart?"

Surprised and overcome by an openness she had never before seen in a man, Tumina embraced Mariano. "Man, your sin is gone," she said, signaling her willingness to reconcile. In so doing, Tumina reflected the reconciliation God was offering to all people everywhere, through His Son.

Back at the translation desk some days later, Mariano told Ken, "You will never know what a wonderful relationship Tumina and I are beginning to have."

ᕦ ᕦ ᕦ ᒐᕤ ᕠ ᕠ ᕠ

IN addition to his role in translation, Mariano proved to be a gifted teacher of the *Good New Words*. Families would come to the Jacobs' compound for medical attention and Chamula believers in the yard would bring them to Mariano to hear the *Good New Words*. One day a man named Vel Gómez Jiménez—better known as Vel Chiotic because he came from the *paraje* of Chiotic—brought his first-born son to the Jacobs' yard. The little boy was sick and his father had heard about the magic machine that can tell you why you were dying.

Like Mariano had been, Vel was a deeply troubled man. *Xbiet ono'ox ti co'ntone*[76]... "My heart never sits down," he told Mariano, meaning *I have no peace in my heart*. As a young man, Vel had tried many things to gain this peace. Every weekend, he went to the caves of Tsonta Vits to fast, pray, and light candles, asking for the gods' favor. He borrowed heavily

---

[76] Literal meaning: "My heart is only and always restless." *Xbiet* means "to be jumping, jumping, jumping."

from his parents and his relatives to buy meat and bread which he placed in the caves for the gods to eat.[77] "I did that for a whole year," reported Vel. "Not only did I still have my burden, but I now had my debt on top of it, at 120 percent interest." Mariano listened patiently.

"Next," Vel said, "I determined to drink the holy *pox*, the gift of the gods, to comfort my heart." He drank heavily and was still unsatisfied. Then he decided he needed a wife, so he purchased a woman at great price from her family. "I was left with an even bigger debt and still no peace, and I found myself hitting my wife in the face and blaming her for my unsettled heart."

Finally Vel told Mariano that he had recently contemplated suicide. He knew just how he would do it. "Up in the high country where I live, there is a river I cross to return home. I've already chosen a tree I could fall out of onto the riverbed below, breaking my head open on the rocks."

About this time, Vel's first-born son had become ill. Deep in debt, he could not afford a shaman's healing ceremony, so he carried the little boy all the way from Chiotic to Elaine's clinic in Las Casas—a five-hour hike.

When Vel finished his story, Mariano began telling this newfound friend his own story, ending with the offer that had brought him peace. One of the first books published in the Chamula language was a compilation of OLD TESTAMENT stories, including the life of Abraham. Mariano used the story of Abraham to explain what had happened in his own life. Vel listened with growing interest.

"I am like Abraham who was an unbeliever," conceded Mariano, as he finished the story. "One day, God came to Abraham and spoke to him in his own language. What other language would God use to speak to Abraham but one he could understand?"

Mariano described how God had made a commitment to Abraham that he and his wife Sarah would have a son, although both were far beyond their child-bearing years. "Abraham simply looked at God and said, 'I take seriously what You have obligated Yourself to do'," explained Mariano. As a result, a son was born to Sarah and Abraham in their old age.

---

[77] Although the food is never physically consumed, Chamulas believe the gods eat the spiritual essence of food offered.

"I am like Abraham," Mariano said again to Vel. "I was an unbeliever who began to hear in my language that God had obligated Himself to take care of my sins and to do for me what I could not do for myself. Like Abraham, I took God seriously."

Mariano repeated it once more. "I am like Abraham," he told Vel. This time he added, "and so are you." Vel got it. He believed the message.

He returned home to his village of Chiotic telling all who would listen, "My search has ended. In these *Good New Words*, I have found medicine for my soul." In the coming years, Vel himself would teach many of his countrymen about the *Good New Words*, and whenever a believing friend would express regret about the trouble he had endured in his early life trying to find peace for his heart, Vel would quickly correct him. "No, my brother, I had to go through all that to learn there was nothing I could do for myself," he emphasized. "It was then I was ready to listen to God."

In the early years of the young, growing Chamula church, the believers also needed counselors to give advice and help resolve disputes. Previously they brought their problems to tribal authorities for resolution, particularly to the president (the man with the mouth). Now outside of Chamula tribal lands, the believers sought leaders in the church for advice. Mariano was one of those leaders.

Early one morning a father and mother brought their fourteen-year-old daughter to Mariano's house. She had been sexually involved with a man to whom she had not been promised, and the parents were seeking counsel.

Sitting on the bench outside his house, Mariano listened to the family as they voiced their concerns. When they finished, he spoke tenderly but authoritatively, using an example from their past to teach them how to live under the government of God. "I have no idea what the answer to your problem is, but I know how you can find a resolution," Mariano began. "When you lived out in Chamula and became sick, remember how you visited a shaman to find out what was killing you? You'd extend your arm to the shaman who would listen to your blood and tell you why you were dying. He would then tell you exactly what color of chicken, how much liquor, what color of candles, and which herbs you must bring him to make you well. Remember how you would buy these things, no matter the cost, and commit yourself totally to the healer?"

Mariano paused. "That is how you must approach God, committing yourself completely to Him, and He will show you the answer to your problem." By pointing to examples from their past traditional approach to life and relating them to principles in the *Good New Words*, Mariano and other leaders helped new believers understand how to live the Christian life.

KEN and Mariano worked together through most of the 1970s to complete the Chamula NEW TESTAMENT. During this decade, the story of God's *Good New Words* transforming hundreds of lives in southern Mexico had reached North America. A book authored by Hugh Steven entitled *They Dared to be Different*[78] tells the story through the life of Mariano. That book touched the hearts of many in the translator's homeland, including someone in Ken Jacobs' own family.

---

[78] **Hugh Steven** (1976), *They Dared to be Different* (Eugene OR: Harvest House Publishers, 160 pages).

14
Back From The Brink

FOR WHAT seemed like the hundredth time in as many days, Dave Jacobs opened the top, right-hand desk drawer in his home office and stared hard at the loaded pistol. Divorced and his career in shambles, the Minneapolis businessman felt particularly vulnerable to temptation that grey, rainy April afternoon in 1980. "No!" he countered, slamming the desk door. "They will not have the satisfaction."

'They' were Dave's business partner and investors, whose nervousness about their floundering machining company had forced Dave to make decisions counter to his self-proclaimed genius. "I was at the top of my accounting and business law classes at the university. Why can't they admit my superior intellect?" questioned the proud man. Dave had achieved his goals of being named controller and vice president at a young age. Dave had also exchanged his belief in the supernatural, for faith in the wisdom of man—particularly his own. Dave spat in frustration.

'They' included his ex-wife, Jan. After twenty years of marriage she'd informed Dave that he no longer loved him. She forced him out of his home and away from his four children. "I don't even have a key for my own house," he grumbled. Sure, he had a reputation for drinking and carousing, having often boasted "there isn't a bar I can't close." But hadn't he also provided a good living for his family, and didn't he deserve an occasional release from the pressures of business?

In Dave's tortured mind, 'they' also included his mother, who died when he was four. 'They' included his demanding father, who was left alone to raise the Iowa farm family's second crop of small children. His father seemed to direct all his anger at stubborn little Dave, who grew up declaring, "I'm not going to be like my dad." The troublemaker gladly left home at age seventeen to make his own way in the world. When anyone asked about his upbringing Dave told them, "My dad was my critic, not my supporter," and quickly changed the subject.

Two decades after leaving the farm, Dave found himself divorced and bankrupt. His only remaining comfort was his live-in girlfriend Susan, who was presently at work. "When I've given up hope," he said, "even her confidence in me is not enough."

Dave got up from his desk and walked down the hallway of their small apartment, trying to get away from the alluring, yet fearful, solution that lay in his desk's top drawer. Seeing his reflection in a mirror at the end of the hall, the distraught man screamed, "Failure!"

It was a term he had once used to describe his older brother Ken, who had moved to Mexico with his wife Elaine almost thirty years ago to translate the Bible for a tribe of Indians. The couple had occupied a special place in Dave's early life. For a year they had suspended their own plans in order to care for the younger siblings, including Dave, while his father recovered from a serious illness. But Dave could never understand his older brother's choice of careers. "A man with your talents and brains should be a productive citizen—and you're sitting down there in the boonies with a bunch of illiterates," he once told Ken. "What's the matter with your head?"

SEEKING distraction from his dark thoughts, Dave wandered into the living room and picked up a book his ex-wife had given him the last time he was home. *They Dared to Be Different*[79] covered the early years of his brother's Bible translation work. "Ken thought you might enjoy reading this," said Jan, half tossing the paperback to Dave in order to avoid physical contact.

---

[79] **Hugh Steven** (1976), *They Dared to be Different* (Eugene OR: Harvest House Publishers, 160 pages).

As he thumbed through the pages and began to read, Dave suddenly began to identify with the book's main character, a Chamula Indian named Mariano whose first wife had been taken from him.

Mariano found himself both rejected by his tribe's traditional system and unable to live by the moral code set forth in the Bible, which he was reading for the first time in his own language. Like Mariano, Dave felt angry, frustrated, and backed into a corner. Most of all, he connected with the Indian man's comment about seeing a dead chicken and envying it. "I know what it's like to envy a dead chicken," mused Dave to himself.

Transfixed by his similarities to Mariano, Dave decided to read the book from cover to cover. Later that day, Dave called Ken. Ken was home temporarily in the United States, but was preparing to return to Mexico. "I've got to see you!" demanded Dave, his voice betraying the desperation in his soul.

Dave hurried over to Ken's place. Ken met him at the door and began with the usual pleasantries—but Dave cut his brother short. "I haven't got time for any of that," he interrupted. "Is it really true there is a living God who wants to involve Himself in my life, to help me make decisions, and to see me succeed?" Dave did not reveal to Ken that he'd already decided in his heart if that kind of God did not exist, then there was no hope, and he didn't want to live.

Is there a living God? What a question to come from Dave, who until that point would have told anyone who asked that he was an atheist—end of conversation. But something Dave read that afternoon had awakened the debate in his soul. Frustrated with his own inability to manage his life, Mariano had talked about finding a new authority in the God of the Bible and in his Son. Out of options, Dave desperately needed the hope this Indian man had discovered half a world away.

Dave poured out to Ken the toxic venom numbing his soul. He described in detail how he'd been wronged by his family, and by his business associates, and by the whole world. Ken listened patiently. His brother's tirade finally ended with these words. "Until now, I've run my own life, and I've run it into a shambles. I've got to have a new authority, like the one Mariano talks about in that book you gave Jan. Can you help me?"

The first words Ken spoke confirmed Dave's worst fears. "There's not a thing I can do to help you."

Then Ken added, "But I know Someone who can." He quoted to Dave the English equivalent of the first BEATITUDE of Jesus as Mariano had helped translate it into the Chamula language: "How wonderful for the person who realizes in his heart that there is nothing he can do to save himself. That person is already being managed by the God of Heaven."[80] Ken knew his younger brother was finally listening.

"Dave," said Ken, "Why don't you pray to God?"

Dave balked. "I never pray," he protested. "I don't know how to pray."

But Ken persisted. "Just tell God exactly what you've been telling me."

So Dave knelt next to a chair and began to talk to that piece of furniture about all the ways people had hurt him and how he couldn't fix things.

By his own admission, Dave did not get far before his solo delivery to an inanimate object was transformed into an astonishing two-way conversation with the God he had rejected since childhood. "It was like He was right there in the room with me," Dave explained later. "Instead of continuing to spew out my anger and hurt, I suddenly became acutely aware of my problem. All those things I had been doing were terrible, and I was killing myself. In reality, I was the problem, and what I needed was forgiveness."

What had begun as accusations quickly turned to confession. "You don't face God and tell Him a bunch of stuff that isn't true," concluded Dave. "Suddenly, truth becomes all important."

Until that evening, it had never dawned on this self-made man that he didn't have the right to use other people. But on that April evening kneeling in the presence of God, Dave realized that this was true. For years he had expected loyalty from all those around him, but he had been loyal to no one but himself. His greatest disloyalty was to God, to whom he was now speaking freely of his failures. Finally, when it seemed he had divulged as much as his tortured mind could endure at one sitting, he heard these words in the depths of his soul: "I know all

---

[80] MATTHEW 5:3/NIV: "Blessed are the poor in spirit, for theirs is the kingdom of heaven." Such English equivalent *back translations*—like the example cited by Ken Jacobs above—are used to check the fidelity of the new indigenous translation compared to the original text.

these things about you Dave. I can forgive and fix you."

A tiny ray of hope pierced the blackness of Dave's depression for the first time in months. Gathering courage from the story of Mariano who made a similar request to God, the broken businessman asked, "I don't know why you would want me, but would you please take over the management of my life?"

"Yes," came the gentle heavenly reply.

Dave does not remember leaving his brother's place that evening; nor did he understand until some time later how the sacrifice of Jesus on the cross made it possible for him to come to God. He does recall that his desire for revenge and suicide—which had nearly overpowered him—was instantly, completely gone.

Dave immediately bought a Bible and began reading it voraciously, like a newborn baby hungry for nourishment. His whole worldview had changed, and Dave desperately needed to know how to live life under this new authority. He even took his Bible on outings to the local Dairy Queen® with Sue. "I'm probably driving her nuts every time I say, 'Listen to what the Bible says about this …'," he thought. But within the year, Sue made a similar profession of faith. Convicted of the need to make their relationship right before God, the couple soon married.

℘ ℘ ℘ ✄ ℘ ℘ ℘

THE impact of Mariano's story did not end there. In the years following his encounter with God, Dave worked as a car salesman at a dealership in the northern suburbs of Minneapolis/St. Paul. He gained the confidence of other broken people, both customers and fellow employees, who needed a new authority in their lives. "I had a way of connecting with people, and the conversation would gravitate naturally to the fact that God is the boss of me," insisted Dave, adding, "Those were the actual words I used."

Dave's openness about his decision to ask God to manage his life gave hope to many others who, in turn, placed their lives under this same New Authority. Dave remembers one customer stating, "If I hadn't met you tonight, I'd be dead tomorrow. I was going to kill myself, and I drove into the dealership to get away from that."

Encounters like this simply confirmed to Dave that God was working through him.

Most importantly, Dave saw both his children and his grandchildren come to faith in Jesus Christ, through prayer and the mercy of God. "I never had it to give them when they were young," he admitted, "but God has loved me and my kids, too." God also healed his relationship with his dad. "He was a devout man," Dave recalled. "I look forward to seeing him again."

Like all believers, Dave has had down times since becoming a believer, but he takes consolation in what God told his Chamula counterpart who once described himself as a man without hope who couldn't keep from doing bad. "God spoke to Mariano and said, 'I'm not going to throw you away. You can and you will do right by means of me'." Living 'by means of God' is how Dave Jacobs now approaches every day as he endeavors to finish well the rest of his life here on earth.

In 2001, Dave Jacobs traveled 1,800 miles south to Chiapas, Mexico, to meet Mariano. The two men embraced and, with Ken interpreting, spent hours sharing the wonder of their redemption and regeneration in Jesus Christ. Dave recalls with crystal clarity what Mariano said concerning the depths to which both had sunk before encountering the Living God. According to Dave, "Mariano got tears in his eyes as he said softly, 'The bottom was a wonderful place to go because it was at that point that change came'."

Both Mariano and Dave can honestly say that God has "lifted me out of the slimy pit, out of the mud and mire; He set my feet on a rock and gave me a firm place to stand" (PSALM 40:2/NIV).

15
That's Real Success

VEL CHIOTIC peered through the bars. For the second time in as many months, he stood inside the jail at San Juan Chamula. At least he had company. His older brother, Agustín, and their cousin, Marcos, had also been arrested again. Vel considered Marcos to be his younger brother, and the three lived a stone's throw from each other in the eastern Chamula village of Chiotic.

"What do we do now?" wondered Agustín.

Vel had an idea. "We've got a hymnal and a guitar," he said, referring to a ukulele Marcos had slung over his back. "Let's sing some songs."

The policemen who knocked at his door earlier that day had ordered Marcos to bring these items with him. "We don't want this evangelical stuff in the village," they barked. Then they marched all three westward to the tribal center—a four-hour walk.

Now behind bars, the prisoners began singing JESUS LOVES ME and other songs of faith that had been translated into the Chamula language.[81] Between songs, Vel, Agustín, and Marcos could hear the bewildered policemen whispering to each other. "These men are in jail. They ought to be afraid of what will happen to them, and here they are singing. Let's listen and see if we can understand what they're singing about."

Vel smiled. "This is God's way of allowing us to witness to our jailers," he thought. "They're posted here to guard us, so they can't leave. We're their captives, but they are captives, too—captives to the *Good New Words*."

[81] By the mid 1970s, the hymnal contained several songs written by Chamula believers themselves.

ℰ ℰ ℰ 𝓍 ℐ ℐ ℐ

In the autumn of 1968, Chamula's president had ordered each tribal family to contribute thirty pesos toward a new municipal headquarters. When no construction took place, three thousand unhappy Chamulas gathered in Las Casas to protest this scam perpetrated by tribal leaders. To avoid a riot, the Mexican government agreed to cover the cost of constructing a new *cabildo* and reimburse each family the tax collected (and squirreled away) by tribal leaders. But the stage was set for confrontation between the populace and the *caciques*.

During the late 1960s, the Roman Catholic Church had launched a movement called *Misión Chamula* with the goal of converting the tribe from its thinly veiled animistic religion to orthodox Catholicism. One of this movement's main tools was the education of young catechists (lay leaders) who would offer religious instruction and courses to improve the lives of Chamula families. By 1969, there were fifteen catechists meeting with more than eight hundred Chamulas—many of them ambitious and frustrated young people who saw little future in a tribe dominated by the *cacique*. These meetings turned into forums for airing grievances about the repressive tribal leadership. By the mid 1970s, several *Misión Chamula* participants had challenged the elders' authority—even running one of the catechists for the office of municipal president and bringing criminal charges against the elders.[82] These charges landed Chamula's principal *cacique* and four of his henchmen in jail. After coercing the judicial system to release the *cacique* and making sure the Mexican government (which depended on the Chamula vote) was solidly in their camp, the elders determined to consolidate their authority. Knowing they could stir traditional Chamulas against religious minorities, they came down hard on the two most visible threats—the practicing Catholics and the new evangelical believers.

Since all Chamulas return to their birth villages on October 31st to celebrate *Todos Santos* (Day of the Dead), the elders chose November 1, 1974, as the day they would expel all dissidents from Chamula. They claimed to have uncovered a plot by Catholic catechists and evangelical leaders and

---

[82] Many traditionalists and a handful of Christian believers, including Miguel Cashlan, were involved in challenging the power of the elders.

their followers to destroy the Church of San Juan Chamula and the saints lining its walls. They convened local councils in twenty-six villages where there were practicing Catholics and/or evangelicals. These councils organized posses which—for three days and nights—systematically dragged both Catholics and evangelicals from their homes. The men were beaten, imprisoned, transported out of the tribal lands, and abandoned. The women and children fled to the woods and took shelter in caves. Eight hundred people (nearly two hundred families) eventually sought refuge in Las Casas.[83]

VEL Chiotic and his brothers had advance warning of the persecution and expulsion. They had heard the rumors tribal leaders were spreading, claiming that Christian believers cannibalize children, participate in drunken orgies, and desecrate the saints and sacred crosses of Chamula. Local villagers assumed these rumors to be true and began to shun and mistreat the believers. It was widely known that something would happen soon to these tribal misfits.

Last year Mariano had explained God's offer to Vel, and in the *Good New Words* the young man from Chiotic had found medicine for his soul. Vel now attended worship services in Las Casas every other weekend. On alternate Sundays, Vel relayed the message he had heard in Las Casas to a handful of believing families who met at his home in Chiotic. Mariano likewise made several trips to visit and encourage the believers in Chiotic. Later, Vel and other young leaders had accompanied Mariano to the villages of Nich´en, Majomut, and Jol Tsemen to teach and encourage believers there. Vel had also attended a spiritual retreat at the Chiapas Bible School in Las Casas,[84] where he met lay leaders from other Tzotzil language groups. Vel's view of the church was expanding and he was growing in effectiveness as a leader. Little wonder that he would be a target of the planned expulsion.

For several weeks prior to *Todos Santos*, the church meeting in Vel's house began preparing for whatever danger might come their way. Believers were praying and fasting one or two days at a time. Rumors circulated that October 31st would be the day. All that day the

---

[83] **Jan Rus** (2005), "The Struggle Against Indigenous Caciques in Highland Chiapas: Dissent, Religion and Exile in Chamula, 1965–1977," *Catiquismo in Twentieth Century Mexico* (Institute for the Americas), pp. 169–192.

[84] The Chiapas Bible School was located on property adjoining *Church of the Divine Redeemer* in Las Casas.

believers waited, and nothing happened. Relieved, they went to bed that night, only to be awakened at 4:30 A.M. the next morning by the sound of people running.

Vel peeked through the crack in his door and saw what looked like a big mass of insects covering the hillside—but the insects were actually people. They were running everywhere and shouting. Men, not only from Chiotic but from various nearby Chamula villages, were assembling outside the believers' homes. A large group stood opposite Vel Chiotic's house and called, "Are you there?" Vel said nothing. "Are you there? Are you there?" the men cried louder and louder.

Vel prayed silently, "Lord, this may be the end for me. I might die now, and I want You to be ready to accept me." He continued to pray in silence.

"Well, he must be there," said a gruff voice, now just outside the door. "Nobody had a chance to leave before we got here." Then Vel heard someone try the door. "It's barred from the inside," complained the voice. "He's got to be in there."

"Let's get a big stone and break the door down," cried another.

Not wanting his house to be damaged, Vel finally replied. "Yes, I'm here. Give me a chance to get dressed and open the door."

When Vel emerged, one of the men shouted, "Bring a rope. We're going to tie him up." But no one had a rope.

"If you need a rope, I've got a new one in the house," offered Vel, adding, "I'll loan it to you." Surprised at this offer, the man with the gruff voice motioned for one of the others to check the house, and he emerged with Vel's new rope. He tried to tie a loop at one end, in order to thread the other end through. After watching the man fumble for a few minutes, Vel finally told him, "Here, let me make the loop for you." To his captors' amazement, Vel grabbed his new rope, fashioned a loop at the end, and gave it back to the man who was charged with tying him up. So with the prisoner's own rope, the man bound Vel like he would a bag of coffee or vegetables, straining mightily to pull the rope tightly through the loop; but Vel felt little discomfort. "Strange," Vel thought to himself, "this isn't tight at all."

The men marched Vel to the school yard in Chiotic. There he saw the Panchins, the Cates, and all the other believing families. Agustín and Marcos were there, too. Like Vel, all the other believers had been bound. During the next several hours their captors taunted and beat them publicly. "You worship the gods of the *cashlan* and now you will know how we feel about your betrayal," bellowed someone in the mob. Others beat the believers with sticks. They beat them with their fists. When their anger finally abated, they marched the believers, blooded and still bound, down the long trail to the tribal center.

Arriving at San Juan Chamula about 4:00 P.M. that afternoon, the believers from Chiotic were unbound, then thrown in jail with believers from three other *parajes*—Jol Tsemen, Majomut, and Nich´en. In all, about one hundred sixty men were crammed into a cell meant for many fewer prisoners. "What is going to happen to us now?" asked one man, panic evident in his voice.

Vel, his heart comforted by the Great Presence, spoke kindly to the man. "Don't worry. We're in God's hands, and if we are in His hands, He will watch over us." To the other believers he said, "Let's just pray together, and God will take care of us." Unable to kneel, for there was only room to stand in that small packed cell, the men began praying and praising the God of the *Good New Words* for His promised protection.

And protect He did.

Around midnight, a figure appeared in the shadows at the rear of the *cabildo*, where only meager jail bars stood between the prisoners and the crisp night air. Uttering a string of curses, the man stuck a gun muzzle between the bars. With no place to go, the horrified prisoners braced themselves for the explosive 'popping' sound that would come a split second prior to the searing pain of bullets penetrating their bodies. 'Click' went the gun, and nothing happened. The man pulled the trigger repeatedly. 'Click, click, click.' Angrily he withdrew his weapon and stalked away. The prisoners comforted each other while giving thanks to God.

Around 2:00 P.M. the following afternoon the men were removed from jail, crammed at gunpoint into two large trucks, and driven outside of Chamula. With standing room only, they endured a two-hour-long drive along the Pan American Highway. Near sunset, their armed drivers finally braked to a stop next to an abandoned sugar cane warehouse. The men were ordered out of the trucks.

"Now you're on the other side of the ocean.[85] You're food for the

---

[85] This was an expression used to describe the huge gulf, not only physically but emotionally, between Chamulas and the land of their birth from which they had been forcibly removed.

Englishmen," sneered one of their captors who informed them they could never come back to Chamula. The drivers climbed back into their trucks and sped away.

"Well, we can't go anywhere tonight, so let's just stay here," said one of the believers. Using the warehouse for shelter, they prayed, talked a bit, and soon fell asleep.

The next morning the *Seguridad Publica* (National Guard) arrived on the scene, bringing chicken, beans, and tortillas for the men to eat. It had been more than two days since they'd eaten, and the men were very grateful for the food. The Guard circled the group of one hundred sixty men to prevent anyone from leaving—yet continued to provide food during the next three days. On the third day, National Guard trucks picked up the men up and brought them back to the edge of San Cristóbal where they were released. The former prisoners quietly made their way to the Jacobs' yard where they were greeted with joy by their wives and children.

BESIDES expelling eight hundred people, tribal traditionalists burned four homes to the ground and uprooted doorposts on many others. Several of the believers' homes were raided. All hymnbooks and copies of Scripture were confiscated or destroyed, along with cassette tape players used to broadcast the *Good New Words*.

The Jacobs allowed many of the displaced Chamulas to build temporary lean-tos and cooking fires in their yard, while the Mexican Presbyterian Church invited others to occupy the grounds of the Chiapas Bible School just a few blocks away. Mexican Presbyterians throughout Chiapas immediately sent food, clothing, and blankets. Within weeks Presbyterian church members throughout Mexico, Canada, and the United States—along with the Reformed Church in America—sent monetary aid. Practicing Catholics and evangelicals experienced the same suffering. In recognition of this suffering, the Catholic Bishop of Chiapas supplied plates, utensils, and blankets for all the expelled Chamulas.[86]

Although they had been warned never to return, a majority of the

---

[86] Greater in number than the evangelicals, the practicing Catholics took refuge in the Jacobs' yard and at the Chiapas Bible School as well. Some of the practicing Catholics eventually resumed their tribal religion, while others joined with the evangelical believers.

evangelical believers gradually filtered back into the tribe. Many returned to plant their fields the following spring. Some, like Vel Chiotic and his brothers, spent only a few weeks in San Cristóbal before testing the authenticity of their enemies' threats by returning home. Little by little they resumed their daily activities and soon began meeting openly for worship.

Whenever Chamula believers experienced strong persecution, they grew stronger in their faith, and more of their countrymen expressed a willingness to 'take seriously' God's offer to manage their lives. Leaders emerged to help in this process. In addition to Mariano, there were seven men, including Vel Chiotic, who ministered to growing flocks in various areas of the tribe. One month after the expulsion, an estimated one-hundred fifty to two hundred believers met for Sunday morning worship in Las Casas. Hundreds of other believers even dared to gather in house churches back in Chamula.

ℰ ℰ ℰ ✤ ᵧ ᵧ ᵧ

As determined as the believers were to return and live their Christianity in front of their fellow Chamulas, the elders were equally determined to rid the tribe of the believers' influence. Two months after returning home to Chiotic, Vel and his brothers were again arrested. Just like before, they found themselves behind bars in San Juan Chamula. Only this time they were serenading the guards thanks to the guitar and hymnal they'd been 'forced' to bring. After a night in jail, the three believers were summoned to appear before the tribal president. All courtesies dispensed, the president's message to Vel, Agustín, and Marcos was unusually blunt.

"Listen to me!" he barked. "You are causing trouble for everyone and no one wants to hear what you are saying. It is not important!"

Vel interrupted, "No, what we have to say is important. God's Word has touched our hearts. We can trust God's Word. The words you say are just like air that comes and goes. They don't mean anything to us, but the *Good New Words* are real."

"You can't talk to me like that!" sputtered the president, rising and grabbing a carbine leaning against his desk. In a rage he pointed the muzzle at Vel's chest and said, "*I'm* the tribal authority. Are you telling me I have no right to kill you?"

Vel spoke carefully and calmly. "You are the president and we respect you. But we respect God more," he began. "If you want to shoot me, you have the right to do that, as the tribal authority. But God also has the right to protect me if He wants. If He wills it, you can shoot that bullet right at me, and it will not hurt me. Or if God wills, you can shoot at me and the bullet will enter my body. I'm flesh and blood, and you can kill me; but it has to be God's will." The president swore as he lowered the gun. His voice hoarse with fury, he ordered the *mayols* to take them to the elders.

The three men had had nothing to eat or drink for twenty-four hours. As they walked across the plaza to face the *moletique*, they wondered how they would be able to talk, as hungry and thirsty as they were. Suddenly a wind blew across the plaza. It swirled around the men, and as it did their hunger disappeared. Later Vel told the believers, "It was like we had just finished eating and drinking. Our stomachs were full and we weren't thirsty anymore."

Refreshed and their spirits renewed, the prisoners proceeded to their meeting with the elders, where they were again threatened and told to stop believing. "We're sorry you do not see us well," said the brothers to the tribal leaders assembled. "We respect you and the traditions, but we now believe the *Good New Words* and must do what God tells us."

After a final warning, the elders released Vel, Agustín, and Marcos, who returned home by way of Mariano's house in Ya'al Vacax.[87] Mariano gave them food and encouraged them to remain faithful.

ᕦ ᕦ ᕦ ᑺ ᕤ ᕤ ᕤ

VEL'S experience was typical of many believers following their 1974 expulsion. Some found work in Las Casas and remained there, but many filtered back into the tribe. As they practiced their newfound faith, believers were often harassed and sometimes beaten by their neighbors. Some, including Vel, were arrested multiple times on a variety of contrived charges. All who identified themselves as evangelical believers were regarded with suspicion. On August 15, 1976, the elders initiated another ruthless campaign to rid the tribe of 'troublemakers.'

---

[87] Despite working in Las Casas with Ken Jacobs on the Bible translation, Mariano had begun to build a home in Chamula. He and others, like Vel Chiotic, believed the best way to respond to persecution was to live and maintain a peaceful witness in tribal lands.

Over a week's time they apprehended, then expelled, about six hundred men, women, and children. Many of the men were beaten. Some of women were raped. Most were evangelical believers, since few practicing Catholics remained in Chamula.

The 1974 and 1976 expulsions marked the beginning of a persecution that would not begin to diminish until the mid-1990s. Though expulsions waxed and waned over this twenty-year period, they occurred with enough frequency that there were always a number of Chamula believers, both families and individuals, who genuinely needed assistance.[88]

After the 1976 expulsion, twelve families ended up in Ken and Elaine Jacobs' yard. Representing these homeless families, a man named Luis approached Ken and Elaine concerning the three hundred linear feet of tin roof, once used as a carport for parked vehicles, which ran along three sides of the Jacobs' walled yard. "May we build temporary shelters under this roof?" The Jacobs assured Luis that the families were most welcome to construct whatever they needed to protect themselves from the cold autumn rains. In the earthen ground beneath the carport, each family scratched boundaries in the dirt to indicate the space they would occupy. They framed each space with old two-by-fours, running from the ground to the roof supports above. They nailed hand-sawed boards to the frames to form walls, and hung old blankets or burlap bags sewn together to serve as doors to their rickety shelters.

Shortly after Luis finished his family's shelter, his wife laid two chairs on their sides, wrapped plastic around them, and placed her straw mat over the hastily constructed bed. Hours later she gave birth on this bed to the couple's third child. Such was life in the refugee camps, both in the Jacobs' yard and at the Chiapas Bible School.

Observing these conditions, one of the last things most people would have said about this particular group of Chamulas was that they were successful. They had lost their homes. They had lost their lands. These losses represented some of their most treasured rights. No longer could they return to the villages of their birth. No longer could they lean forward and receive the touch from the back of a tribal elder's right hand on their foreheads—a sign of tribal acceptance.

Despite severe hardships, most believers maintained positive atti-

[88] **Alan John Schreuder** (June 2001), *A History of the Rise of the Chamula Church*—Master's Thesis (Pasadena CA: Fuller Theological Seminary, School of World Mission and Institute of Church Growth), p. 99.

tudes. "I have not heard one call for revenge," wrote Ken Jacobs in a letter to his supporters. "Almost every day, I hear the Chamulas talking about the value of suffering. There is also much prayer, and even tears, for their enemies. Obviously, God is ministering to them in the present situation."

On a particularly dreary day in late October 1976, Luis and other Chamula men gathered together on the muddy ground of this tiny refugee camp. Their clothes were in tatters. A cold rain dripped through the tin roofs of their makeshift shelters, dribbling onto what little they had salvaged from their now-abandoned Chamula homes. The scene appeared tragic. Yet these men talked excitedly of something greater than their present discomfort. From across the yard Ken approached the group, but stopped short and pulled out the notepad he always carried. As a translator of the language, he was intensely interested in how Chamulas expressed themselves, but he did not want to interrupt their conversation. He merely listened from a distance. What Ken heard and wrote in his notepad that grey fall day was this: *Naca sta ta jtatic ti c´usi oy ta yo´nton ti Dios ta jtojoltique*. . . "We are in the process of attaining what God has in His heart as it pertains to us,"[89] Luis told the other men, who nodded in agreement.

"Wow!" Ken thought to himself. "Now that's *real* success!"

A less literal translation of Luis' statement might have been, "We are gaining God's goal for our lives." Somehow, in the midst of extreme poverty, rejection, mud, and uncertainty, these Chamula Christians had grasped a great truth, a truth which transcended their present circumstances and radically transformed their spiritual lives. No longer were they enslaved to the holy *pox*, to the dreadful power of shamans, to *cargos* that kept them perpetually poor, to the demands of their capricious ancestral gods, nor to their own propensity to sin. They were being governed by the God of Heaven, Who had made Himself their benefactor and Who had delivered them from their enemies. Stripped of everything, the believers looked forward to all God had promised them in the *Good New Words* concerning this life and the next. More than that, they considered those promises already in hand!

---

[89] This expression is similar to the Chamula expression for *hope*. When referring to that unseen but certain expectation of God's promises that accompanies repentance and faith, a Chamula will say, *jpatoj co´nton ti ta jtatic ti c´usi yalojbotic ti Dios ti ta xiyac´botique*. . . "I have comforted my heart that I will get that which God has said He will give us."

16
Finding Their Place

THE 1976 EXPULSIONS marked a turning point concerning the future of the Chamula believers and of the city of San Cristóbal de Las Casas. With the tribal elders' entrenched position and little support from the Mexican government, many *expulsados* gave up their dreams of ever returning to live in Chamula. This change in mindset began a cultural transformation that would forever alter the lives of both the indigenous Indian peoples of the central highlands and the Ladinos occupying the Valley of Jobel.

Soon after the August 16th expulsion, several leaders among the Chamula believers, with support from the Mexican Presbyterian Church, purchased four hectares[90] of land on the northeastern edge of San Cristóbal. The land was parceled out to families wishing to build new homes. The first houses were constructed, effectively creating a new colony eventually named *Nueva Esperanza* (New Hope). Though it may have looked like mere shacks to the old Spanish families ruling the city, Nueva Esperanza represented a fresh start for the believers, many of whom had already found jobs laying brick, gardening, or unloading trucks in the Las Casas marketplace. Others started small businesses to serve their fledgling community. After finishing their homes, they constructed a church building and then a school.

The establishment of Nueva Esperanza represented the breaking of a racist barrier against Indian residence within the city of San Cristóbal de Las Casas. As late as 1952 it was illegal for a Chamula or any

---

[90] One hectare is 10,000 square meters, or 2.471 acres.

person of indigenous heritage to be found in the city after sunset. That law had been formally revoked, but Ladinos continued to discriminate by expecting the Indians to step aside on sidewalks and refusing to sit next to them in public places. For their part, Indians preferred not to stay overnight in the city.[91]

Now, for the first time, Chamulas had gained a toehold in Las Casas because of their great need and because a recognized Mexican church had become their advocate. No doubt the city fathers congratulated themselves on their compassion in approving the sale of this marginal land. Perhaps they viewed Nueva Esperanza as a temporary settlement at best, knowing the strong emotional pull of the Chamula homeland. Their view would soon change radically as the believers established even more colonies. The continuing growth of the Chamula church and the expulsion of confessing believers from the tribe—one thousand by the end of 1976, and three thousand by 1980—soon filled Nueva Esperanza to capacity. By 1981 land for three more *colonias* had been purchased along the Pan American highway south of the city: *Betania* (Bethany), *Galilea* (Galilee) and *Vista Hermosa* (Beautiful View).

Other colonies would soon encircle Las Casas as more Chamulas poured into the valley, followed by refugees from other indigenous people groups. Those who settled in the new colonies around Las Casas were perceived to be better off economically. This perception and the continuing persecution of believers in Chamula and other Tzotzil language groups opened the flood gates of migration to a city which had extended a reluctant hand to the first Chamula believers.[92]

MIGUEL Cashlan proved to be an able leader and administrator for the community of the *expulsados* in their early years. Having spent much of his life in the Spanish-speaking world, he was an effective communicator with the Ladino community. Miguel also had established legal and governmental contacts that served Chamula believers well as

[91] **Jan Rus** (2007), *The New Mayan City in the Valley of Jovel: Rapid Urbanization, Indigenous Youth, and Community in San Cristóbal de las Casas* (Riverside CA: Latin American Studies), pp. 9–10.

[92] *Ibid.*, pp. 11–14.

they fashioned new lives in the city. For these refugees who no longer had the support of their traditional leadership, Miguel became 'the man with the mouth' and the one to whom they looked for guidance in rebuilding their lives outside of their original Chamula tribal lands.

According to Chamula tradition, a leader who takes the people in a new direction is responsible for what results. Miguel was one of the first six believers who had encouraged others to consider the claims of God on their lives. Little wonder that he would shoulder the burden of those who, by embracing Christianity, had lost everything.

"You're responsible for this," the people would say—not maliciously, but matter-of-factly. "You brought us the *Good New Words* and so you must address the needs of all these people."

Consequently it was Miguel, together with the Caxtuli brothers and other early believers, who made sure each family had housing and food. When the church met for worship he would ask, "How many have been driven out of their villages this week? Is anybody hungry?" Those who had recently arrived would raise their hands and the leaders would take down their names and provide beans, corn, and salt to tide them over until they could find work. In that way, the Chamula church behaved much like the early Christian church as recorded in the ACTS OF THE APOSTLES. Although Chamulas never divided property as the early Jewish believers did, no one went hungry and everyone had a roof over their heads.

It was Miguel and other 'first Christians' who negotiated the purchase of land on which Nueva Esperanza was built. When a Chamula had a question concerning interpretation of the Biblical text, he would go to Miguel's son Mariano. But issues of administrative or political significance were directed to Miguel, who many addressed as *Mol* Miguel, a title reserved for respected Chamula elders.

Before Miguel had come to believe the *Good New Words*, he had been an abusive father to his son Mariano. As a result there was little respect between father and son. As a small boy, Mariano was clothed in rags and was always cold because his father drank away their money. During Mariano's formative years, Miguel had pushed his son away by calling him 'worthless' and 'a stupid goat.' He criticized everything Mariano tried to do, taking out his personal frustrations on the boy and his mother, both of whom he beat regularly.

"No matter what I do," Mariano told his grandmother one day after Miguel berated the lad for holding a machete incorrectly, "I cannot attain the love of my father. I live now only by hating him."[93] When Mariano was older, Miguel forced Mariano to work with him on the coffee plantations but kept everything his son earned.

Now an adult, Mariano shared a common faith with his father, but wounds from their earlier relationship had not been healed. Add to that the fact that both Miguel and Mariano saw different paths for the Chamula believers. Miguel was convinced they should work through Mexico's judicial system to rectify the wrongs of the traditionalists against the believers, while Mariano believed Scripture taught believers to turn the other cheek. Both rose as leaders of two different factions within the group of expulsed believers. These groups worshiped separately and members of Miguel's congregation, which was larger, often belittled Mariano's abilities as a leader. In turn, Mariano had spoken spiteful things against his father.

During the expulsions of the mid-1970s, Ken and Mariano continued to translate the *Good New Words*. As the decade drew to a close and the entire NEW TESTAMENT was ready for press, the Chamula believers planned a big celebration at which the first copies of the Scriptures would be distributed to each family. But Mariano could not bring himself to celebrate. The hate he had secretly nurtured, despite his acceptance of God's offer, had sapped his joy. He was clearly out of fellowship with the God and the *Good New Words* he'd been recommending to others.

AFTER completing the NEW TESTAMENT translation, Ken and Elaine Jacobs moved from Chiapas to the Mexican State of Hidalgo to administer Wycliffe's Linguistics Center at Ixmiquilpan. Mariano and Tumina had purchased two lots in the new colony of Betania and were preparing to build their home there. Like the Jacobs' yard where the couple had lived during their years of translation, their Betania property was populated with trees. Mariano loved these trees. When he wasn't working as night

---

[93] **Hugh Steven** (1976), *They Dared to be Different* (Eugene OR: Harvest House Publishers), p. 30.

watchman at a BFGoodrich Tires® dealership in Las Casas or pastoring his church, he was out clearing his property and pruning his beloved trees.

One day Mariano and Tumina were both working on their land in Betania. As the couple attempted to dislodge a dead branch from one of the trees, suddenly the limb broke loose and fell on Mariano's leg, fracturing it. Mariano refused to be taken to a hospital. "That's where they cut your legs off," he protested. Instead, a neighbor crudely set the bone and men from his church fashioned a stretcher to carry him back to Las Casas.

For weeks Mariano lay staring at the ceiling and bemoaning all that was wrong with his life. In pain, out of money, and out of fellowship with God, he was all alone—or so he told himself. Some Christian Chamulas, envious of his position in leadership and his role as the translator's helper, were gleeful at his misfortune. "I hope he never walks again," some had said. This fed Mariano's self-doubt and rekindled his anger at what he considered the source of his failures—his father, Miguel. But the Great Presence was at work in his disability. As He had earlier, God used a low point in Mariano's life to expand the young man's understanding of His sovereignty.

Immobile and with ample time on his hands, Mariano began reading a Spanish version of the OLD TESTAMENT and doing the work of a translator by mentally converting those words to the language of his heart. In the book of DEUTERONOMY, Mariano read Moses' prediction that there would come a time when the Children of Israel would abandon God and worship false gods. Then, in times of trouble when all their strength is gone, Israel will look in vane for these false gods to deliver them. Speaking through Moses in Chapter 32, the Lord mocks his wayward children:

NOW WHERE ARE THEIR GODS, THE ROCK THEY TOOK REFUGE IN, AND THE GODS WHO ATE THE FAT OF THEIR SACRIFICES AND DRANK THE WINE OF THEIR DRINK OFFERINGS? LET THEM RISE UP TO HELP YOU! LET THEM GIVE YOU SHELTER! (VS. 37–38/NIV).

Suddenly Mariano saw himself clearly. Like Israel, he had been sacrificing to false gods—the gods of pride and of self pity—as he allowed his present circumstances and his critics to nurse his past injuries into a destructive fire. Mariano continued reading:

SEE NOW THAT I MYSELF AM HE! I PUT TO DEATH AND I BRING TO LIFE. THERE IS NO GOD BESIDES ME. I HAVE WOUNDED AND I WILL HEAL, AND NO ONE CAN DELIVER OUT OF MY HAND (VS. 39).

Mariano began to comprehend a terrible—but freeing—truth. He wasn't just angry at his father, at his injury, at the church for not helping him financially when he was down, and at those Chamulas who wished him ill. He was, in fact, angry at God for permitting these things to happen. He was not fully trusting God to manage his life—to be his benefactor, no matter what happened. Mariano knew he had to make a choice. He could hold onto his grievances and continue to wallow in self pity, or he could let them go and accept the Almighty's sovereignty in his life.

Mariano lifted his right hand toward heaven and in one word surrendered to whatever it would be that God would do in his life. *Jechuc*,[94] he said. "Let it be so." With perhaps the shortest prayer he'd ever prayed, Mariano acknowledged God as *God*, and became a changed man from that day forward.

Father and son reconciled just days before the NEW TESTAMENT dedication. Mariano asked his father's forgiveness for criticizing Miguel in the presence of other believers. In return, Miguel spoke words Mariano had been longing to hear. "Son I forgive you with all my heart. Forgive my poor example. I didn't do right when you were small. Forgive me."[95]

꧁ ꧂ ꧁ 🙶 ꧂ ꧂ ꧂

A SEA of blue greeted late arrivals to the site of the big celebration at Nueva Esperanza on January 2, 1980. The brilliant sky seemed to reflect the bright blue shawls of several hundred Chamula women crowded together on the grass in front of the platform where Miguel and other leaders prepared to dedicate the blue-covered books inscribed *Ti Ach´ Rextomento Yu´un Ti Jesucristoe* (THE NEW TESTAMENT ABOUT JESUS CHRIST). Every able-bodied resident of New Hope Colony had pitched in to clear the land, to build a platform, and to install a makeshift

---

[94] **Jechuc** — the equivalent of *Amen* in the English language.

[95] **Larry Clark** (May/June 1980), "We'll Stand Together," *Other Words*, Wycliffe Bible Translators, pp. 1–3.

covering from an old parachute.

This new day coincided with an annual festival celebrated in old Chamula—the changing of tribal authorities. The 3,000 Chamula Christians and their guests meeting on this day were celebrating a new authority in their lives—the government of God.

"In the past, we didn't know God," they told each other, as they labored to put the celebration together. "Now we have His *Good New Words*." The Chamula NEW TESTAMENT was now a reality, and soon each family would receive a copy.

Seventy-five Chamula women had risen at 1:00 A.M. to start the cooking fires needed for the festival. Fourteen huge wash tubs held simmering soup brimming with meat and vegetables. Eighty men had also gotten up early. They hauled firewood and butchered two bulls which provided meat and flavoring for the soup. A fifty-gallon drum sparkled with refreshing green Kool-Aid®, replacing the traditional *pox* that dominated previous festivals in old Chamula.

The Chamula believers shouldered the entire cost of the feast, nearly 24,000 pesos.[96] Believers from other Tzotzil tribes had also come to the celebration, some hiking long hours to attend. They arrived hungry and tired, but full of enthusiasm for the work God had done in the lives of their Chamula brothers and sisters.

During the four-hour ceremony, many of the believers spoke. Vel Chiotic, jailed many times for his faith, urged the assembly, "Enjoy and obey the Word of God." Nicholas, the Huisteco believer who had encouraged the first Christians expulsed from Chamula, told the crowd, "We rejoice that the Word is also in the Chamula tongue." Xun, a man who had suffered greatly for his faith, stood fearlessly before his people and declared the power of God's Word: "The elders once dragged me to jail with a rope around my neck," he said, adding with a smile, "but the Word of God can't be bound." Domingo and Mariano, early believers and Ken's helpers in the translation effort, looked on with thanks in their hearts to God.

Near the end of the ceremony, Ken and Elaine each stood and addressed the assembly. The NEW TESTAMENT translation was complete,

---

[96] Each believer had agreed to contribute two weeks wages to the celebration. In 1980, 24,000 pesos was equivalent to about $3,000 U.S. dollars—a large sum for the young church.

and they were saying goodbye to a people they had grown to love, though by now the body of believers was so great they could not know everyone personally. Still, Elaine saw many familiar faces in the crowd. "Many of you came to me or brought your babies to me for medical attention, and I am so thankful I could be there," she said.

In his farewell address to the Chamulas with whom he'd labored more than twenty years to translate the NEW TESTAMENT, Ken read from ACTS 20:32/NIV: "Now I commit you to God and the word of His grace, which can build you up and give you an inheritance among all those who are sanctified."

Then came the moment all had been waiting for. The heads of each Chamula family quickly formed a line extending one-half block long and pushed eagerly forward to purchase their family's copy of the Chamula NEW TESTAMENT. Twenty years ago, Chamulas showed little interest in God's Word. Now they were hungry to read what God was saying to them in their own language. Within a short time, the first shipment of five hundred copies was sold out.[97]

As Ken watched the life-giving drama unfolding before his eyes, another Chamula believer stepped to his side. As if to put the scene in perspective for the translator, the man nudged Ken. "Brother Canuto," he whispered, excitedly, "Look at the harvest which has resulted from the planting of God's Word by you and Elena."

Ken reflected on this. "If we've helped the Chamulas find God," he thought to himself, "then they have enriched our lives even more so. Their simple faith, their deep insight into God's Word, and their total commitment to Christ shames us, and makes us reach out to God that he might do the same for us."

OFTEN during the years that Ken and Elaine spent attending to medical needs and working to learn the right words to translate the NEW TESTAMENT, their Chamula friends would ask, "Canuto, how do you and

---

[97] The Chamulas immediately ordered an additional 2,000 copies of the Chamula NEW TESTAMENT from the publisher, the World Home Bible League.

Elena live? You don't have a cornfield. How do you eat?"

Then Ken would explain. "There are people in North America who love and pray for you. But that's not all they do," he continued. "They sent Elena and me here to translate the *Good New Words* for you, and they are the ones who buy our beans and tortillas."

Soon after the completion of the NEW TESTAMENT, a delegation of Chamula church leaders and believers presented the Jacobs with a letter they had written to the believers from the United States who had supported the translation effort. In part, the letter read:

> "BECAUSE YOU HAVE A GOODNESS OF HEART SIMILAR TO THAT IN THE HEART OF OUR LORD JESUS CHRIST, YOU FELT IT TO BE OF EXTREME IMPORTANCE TO SEND TO MEXICO KEN AND ELAINE JACOBS WHO WERE CHOSEN BY GOD TO DO THE WORK OF TRANSLATING GOD'S WORD FOR US. NOW, THE ENTIRE NEW TESTAMENT HAS BEEN TRANSLATED INTO OUR CHAMULA LANGUAGE, AND WE ARE ABLE TO SAY THAT WE, THE CHAMULAS OF CHIAPAS, HAVE IN OUR POSSESSION AND IN OUR OWN LANGUAGE THE WORD OF GOD.

> "BEFORE THE COMING OF THE SCRIPTURES, YEAR AFTER YEAR PASSED, AND WE NEVER KNEW WHAT GOD HAD TO SAY TO US. NOW WE CHAMULA INDIANS IN LARGE NUMBERS ARE HEARING GOD SPEAK. WE HAVE COME TO KNOW OF FORGIVENESS OF OUR SINS; WE NOW KNOW THAT GOD SEES US WELL THROUGH JESUS CHRIST AND WHAT HE HAS DONE; AND WE HAVE COME TO KNOW THAT WE HAVE NEW LIFE THROUGH JESUS CHRIST.

> "THEREFORE, BRETHREN, ACCEPT OUR GREETINGS AND THANKS AS PAYMENT FOR WHAT YOU HAVE DONE FOR US. FOR, IN REALITY, THIS IS ALL WE HAVE WITH WHICH TO PAY YOU. WE HAVE NO SILVER OR GOLD. THE ONLY THING WE HAVE TO EXTEND TO YOU IS *COL A VAL*... 'THANK YOU'!"

17
Hungry For God's Word

THE BELIEVERS prospered in their new communities outside of Chamula, but they did not stop being Chamulas. The men and women who established the first four colonies on the edge of San Cristóbal and south along the Pan American Highway did not give up their dress or their Maya way of life. Although they had been permitted to settle near a major Ladino city, a great deal of prejudice still existed toward all Indians. Consequently the newcomers supported one another and celebrated their heritage, rather than assimilating and trying to become Ladinos.

The organization of these early colonies around their common beliefs also gave the residents cohesion. Their spiritual and cultural center was the church, and a place for that church to meet was usually the first public building to be constructed. The founders of Nueva Esperanza built a large house of worship soon after the community was established. The Chamula believers raised and paid for the walls, while Spanish-speaking Presbyterians throughout the state of Chiapas contributed the roof. This further solidified the believers' relationship with the Mexican Presbyterian Church. Most early believers affiliated with the Presbyterian denomination, although a handful of believers identified with the Seventh Day Adventists. Pentecostal congregations grew rapidly during the 1980s and 1990s.

While they kept primarily to themselves, the believers made a favorable impression on the Ladinos who initially employed them as common laborers. Chamulas had been known as hard workers since the 16th Century when Spain conscripted labor from the tribe to build the city's magnificent Roman Catholic church buildings. But Chamula believers were also polite and honest workers who paid their utility bills and mortgages on time. And since they no longer drank *pox* or bore the financial burden of tribal *cargos*, they could save some of what they earned. Many believers soon formed their own service businesses or purchased stalls in the city marketplace to sell goods others had produced, in addition to their own.[98]

No story illustrates the transformation in the believers' economic fortunes quite like that of Sebastián Hernández Caxtuli, the father of Manuel and Tumin. The brothers were among the first to follow the *Good New Words*. Along with his family, Sebastián was driven from his home in 1974 with only a small sack of corn on his back. He spent many weeks as a refugee in the Jacobs' yard. When he left the tribe, Sebastián was a thin man, physically weakened by years of drinking and fighting tuberculosis which produced frequent coughing spells. To make a living, the elder Caxtuli had borrowed money to buy raw peanuts. He roasted them on a barrel top in the Jacobs' yard, then sold each handful for a peso or two.

Visiting the Presbyterian Church in Nueva Esperanza years later, Ken and Elaine Jacobs reunited with Sebastián, whom they described as "much heavier and more robust than the first time we met him." Sitting at the front of the congregation, Sebastián sang the hymns with gusto, though he had never learned to read Chamula and could not follow along in the hymnbook. After the service, Sebastián and his wife Xunca invited the Jacobs to their newly constructed home in New Hope.

Entering the house, Ken and Elaine found Sebastián perched on a small chair by the fire. Behind him was a mound of raw peanuts in sacks piled to the ceiling. "Brother Canuto," began Sebastián. "Did you hear what the pastor said this morning? He said, 'Christ will restore everything that is lost to the one who follows him'." The old man turned and pointed to the wall of peanuts, which Ken estimated at 40,000 pesos in

[98] **Jan Rus** (2007), *The New Mayan City in the Valley of Jovel: Rapid Urbanization, Indigenous Youth, and Community in San Cristóbal de las Casas* (Riverside CA: Latin American Studies), pp. 13–15.

NOTE: *Valley of Jovel* may also be spelled with a "b" as in *Valley of Jobel*; "b" is what we use throughout this book.

value. "Look at all of these peanuts—and *all* of them are paid for," grinned Sebastián, gratefully adding, "God keeps His Word."

Sebastián's story was typical of those who fled Chamula in the early years. Several of the early believers became entrepreneurs who invested in land and established additional colonies to accommodate the increasing flow of Chamulas and other Tzotzil-speaking peoples into the city. After a major economic downturn in 1982, the believers' success stories and the ongoing persecution in Chamula drove more and more of their countrymen into the Valley of Jobel. The Indian population of San Cristóbal increased from 3,000 to 20,000 during the 1980s, and the number of mostly indigenous colonies on the city's outskirts grew from four to sixteen.[99]

THE success enjoyed by expelled Chamula believers was well known to the tribal elders. Besides being an embarrassment to the traditional system from which the *caciques* profited, the growing community of believers now residing in Las Casas continued to spread their odious message throughout the tribe. As fast as believers were expelled, house churches sprang up formed by new converts. This regeneration occurred as displaced believers traveled back into the tribe to visit relatives and friends, or in the more tolerant *parajes* as believers returned to plant their crops and live at least part-time. The *Good New Words* also spread as tribal members traveled to Las Casas on business, stopping by Nueva Esperanza to visit expelled friends and relatives.

Unable to prevent the *Good New Words* from penetrating the tribe, the elders contrived to silence the most visible advocate of the message. They were still smarting from Miguel Cashlan's personal involvement with one of the political parties which tried to subvert the elders' iron grasp on the tribal presidency. They had also tired of endless legal battles with Miguel and other activists who took the battle over the expelled Chamulas' land rights as high as the federal government in faraway Mexico City.

[99] **Jan Rus** (2005), *Caciquismo in Twentieth Century Mexico* (London: Institute for the Study of The Americas), pp. 179–199.

"Perhaps if we remove the head of this serpent, the body will stop writhing," said a *cacique*, referring to the outcasts who claimed Miguel as their respected leader. The Little Brothers of San Juan[100] nodded their consent.

On a late summer afternoon in 1981, as Miguel walked along the main road from Las Casas carrying a cardboard carton of bread to sell in his store in Nueva Esperanza, a car pulled alongside. Four strong men jumped out and grabbed Miguel. They beat the 70-year-old man with clubs, forced him into the car, and sped off.

His abductors took Miguel to the village *Milbil Tulan* (Killed Oak) where they tortured and killed him. Some say he was hacked apart by machetes. Others claim he was bludgeoned with ice picks. Still others insist he was hanged. Las Casas police eventually located Miguel's mutilated body and returned it to Nueva Esperanza for burial. Instead of deflating the believers, Miguel's killing had the opposite effect. The outrageous act generated solidarity among the believers who considered Miguel a martyr for his faith. It was widely reported that he shouted, as he was forced into the car on the day of his death, "You have my body. Do with it as you please, but you will never touch my soul."

TWENTY-seven-year-old María Pérez López and Juan López Ic´alnabil moved slowly along with the throng of thousands winding their way through the streets of Las Casas in the funeral procession for Mol Miguel. Not only the Christian Chamulas, but other Tzotzil- and Tzeltal-speaking peoples and representatives of the Ladino community came to pay their respect to this champion of faith and freedom. They may not have always agreed with his methods, but they could not deny that Miguel's passion for the well-being of all indigenous refugees had helped countless individuals and had changed the face of the city of Las Casas.

María herself had not always believed. Long before her mid-1970s expulsion from Jol Tsemen, the village of her birth, María was distraught and angry at family members who were beginning to follow the

---

[100] The elders referred to themselves as the *Little Brothers of San Juan*, meaning those who are alive and charged with keeping the traditions of the ancestors. *San Juan* is the patron saint of Chamula.

Good New Words. Her cousin Losha López Ic´alnabil had lost a daughter, niece, and nephew in the 1967 attack on Paxcu and the children. "Why does my older sister[101] [cousin] believe what she believes?" questioned María, sick at the loss of the children. "This is what killed Tumina in the fire and Domingo with a machete!"

Three years after that attack, María became gravely ill while her husband was in the 'hot country,' working on a coffee *finca.* For three months María was bedridden. "I'm going to die," she moaned. In desperation her thoughts turned to her cousin Losha, whom she heard was *walking well*[102] in San Cristóbal de Las Casas. Losha had lived there since the deaths of the children. "I need to ask her help," resolved María. With great effort, she rose from her bed and walked from Jol Tsemen to Las Casas in one day, making her way to her cousin's home in the *barrio* of San Nicolás.

For three weeks, Losha nursed María, feeding her chicken, beef, or whatever she asked for, and telling her about the God of the *Good New Words.* "If you believe in Jesus as your Lord and Savior," claimed her cousin with unwaivering certainty, "if you trust Him with all of your heart, you will be healed." María decided to believe.

She got stronger, recovered from her illness, and returned to Chamula as a believer. Her husband Juan, however, was enslaved to alcohol and feared the recrimination of the tribe. Not until three years later did he place his faith in Jesus. A short time later, just prior to All Saints Day, María and Juan were forced to give up their home and take refuge in Las Casas. There they found fellowship with a small group of expulsed Christians meeting in the yard of the Chiapas Bible School on *Calle Ejercito Nacional* (National Army Street). They worshipped with these believers and studied the *Good New Words* under Vel Chiotic, who encouraged María to become involved in doing God's work.

Although in the traditional system Chamula women remained silent at civic and religious events, leaders of the early Chamula church recognized María's ability to speak God's Word prophetically to both men and women, and to pray for the sick. She accompanied Vel Chiotic

---

[101] Chamulas often refer to extended family members of the same generation as sisters or brothers.

[102] **Walking Well** — the English equivalent to an Indian expression meaning *prospering* or *doing well.*

and others to the *parajes* of Ya´alboc, Pinar, and Abretasa where they shared the *Good New Words*. Soon people from many of these villages began pouring into the yard at the Chiapas Bible School. "Most of them had sicknesses and required some form of healing," said María, who prayed with many of them. "They began to believe in Jesus, too, and very soon filled the whole yard on Ejercito Nacional."

One of the first to approach María for prayer was a woman whose husband was an alcoholic and had frequently beaten her, and now had another woman. María counseled the woman, "Believe with all your heart that God can resolve your problems, and He will." The woman believed, and followed María's instructions as to how to respond to her husband. As María had predicted, in just one day the man turned from his illicit relationship and returned to his wife. At the husband's request, the wife invited María to their home to pray with him for delivery from alcoholism. "You only need to pray to the Lord Jesus Christ to be free of your vices," declared Maria. The husband prayed—and he stopped drinking. Before she left, María told him, "Some day, if this is what God wants, you might even become a servant of God." The man, Mateo Hernández Xilon, eventually became a preacher of the *Good New Words* in Nueva Esperanza.

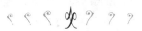

THE line to view the body of Miguel Cashlan stretched for miles down the narrow streets of New Hope. María and Juan had waited in this line for what seemed like hours, when to their surprise Mateo's familiar face appeared at the side of the street. The man greeted Juan and María, his spiritual mother, then soberly requested their assistance. "My nephew, Pax, is dying," said Mateo. "Would you come and visit him?" The couple immediately relinquished their place in the funeral line and followed Mateo to his brother's home.

Mateo's brother, Tin Hernández Xilon, had moved his family from Chamula to the city of Las Casas to escape poverty in their home village of Pozuelo and to make it possible for his son Chus to continue schooling. Tin was not a Christian, and when he had money, he squandered it on liquor. But he loved fifteen-year-old Chus and his two younger sons, Juan and Pax.

Soon after moving to the Las Casas *barrio* of Santa Cruz, Pax became very ill. The family had already experienced great tragedy. Five other sons had each fallen ill and died. So Tin went to the marketplace to find a shaman who could help them. The shaman arrived at the family's home, lifted Pax's wrist and felt the boy's pulse. "There is nothing I can do for him," he announced, matter-of-factly. "It is time to make up your mind whether you will bury your son here or out in the village."

Upset at the prospect of losing yet another son, Tin made the reluctant decision to seek help from his brother, Mateo. Tin had heard that people for whom evangelical believers pray are often healed, but he also knew that Mateo had been driven out of his *paraje*, losing his land, his house, and all his belongings. "I don't want to be associated with an evangelical, because the same thing could happen to us," worried Tin, who still owned a house and property in Chamula. "On the other hand, my son is going to die, and I've already lost five sons. What do we have to lose?"

Having experienced the power of prayer in his own life, Mateo sent María López to the bedside of the young Pax. She prayed for the boy, and the sickness left him. At the same time, she explained to Tin and his family about the God who heals. "Jesus is the one who can heal, and He can also change your lives," she told them. Tin, his wife Dominga, and their sons Chus, Juan, and Pax decided to follow Jesus and began attending worship services at the Chiapas Bible School.

A short time later the family returned to their tribal home to celebrate All Saints Day with their relatives. But news had already reached their village that they had become evangelicals. Local officials arrested Tin and Dominga, and took them to the town center for questioning. When they couldn't convince the couple to renounce their Christian faith, they escorted the family to the tribal center. There Tin was forced to sign a paper stating he was leaving Chamula voluntarily and renouncing any claims on his land and other possessions.

"Our family had to walk back into Las Casas from San Juan Chamula and our rented house in Santa Cruz became our home," recalls Tin's son, Chus, who later succeeded Vel Chiotic as pastor of a church in the colony of believers named *Getsemani* (Gethsemane). Juan and María López, both now in their seventies, attend that church today.

૨ ૨ ૨ ✿ ૭ ૭ ૭

As the sheer number of believers grew, so did their hunger for the *Good New Words*. Almost immediately after the dedication of the Chamula NEW TESTAMENT, Ken Jacobs, assisted by a team of Chamula language helpers, began work on a revised version that was completed in December of 1984. The Chamula church, which at that point consisted of more than 10,000 adult Christians, requested 15,000 copies of the revision.

How easy it would have been for men judged worthy of translating the Bible to put themselves on a pedestal. No doubt leaders of the congregations who selected the Chamula translation helpers thought highly of such men. Yet looking day after day into the Word of God in the effort to transfer it accurately and effectively from one language to another, had life-changing consequences for some, as Mariano Cashlan could attest. For others, it brought back haunting memories of life without Christ. Here is Ken Jacobs' account of one man involved in the Chamula NEW TESTAMENT revision.

"We had finished our translation work for the day. Our heads were bowed, and it was Fortunato's turn to close the day in prayer. Fortunato was the oldest man on the committee, except for me. His friendly grin, revealing a missing front tooth, gave the impression he was younger than his forty-eight years. Soaking wet he'd barely weigh one hundred twenty-five pounds. The serenity he now expressed as a believer stood in sharp contrast to the restlessness that once stormed his life. Powerful witchdoctors and fickle Chamula gods were the mystical forces that ruled his complex tribal religious past. Inside Fortunato in those days, things were quite different. Somewhere, there must be something or someone that could calm this restlessness.

"Suddenly Fortunato's muffled sobs broke the stillness of the room. Our team had just finished revising the Scripture in LUKE Chapter Eight that concerns Jesus' encounter with the demon-possessed man from the region of Gadarenes who was living in the village cemetery. The villagers had bound the madman, for their protection or his, but he was constantly breaking those bonds. Could it be that Fortunato was reflecting on the similarity of that madman's life to his own? As the members of our translation team explored this passage, we could almost hear the clanging chains the neighbors dragged along to bind their dangerous friend, and the long, restless hours this poor devil-driven soul scraped his shackles against sharp tombstones to gain his empty freedom. Oh, what a relief he experienced when Jesus freed him.

"Now, Fortunato's muffled sobs turned to uncontrolled weeping. Slowly he fought his emotions into stubborn submission. Respectfully, he began to talk to the Friend of the Gadarene. 'Oh Lord, how well You remember how I, too, used to ask in my heart, "Where, oh where, is there help?" And there was no help—only the harsh unsatisfying counsel of the shamans. But how well You remember, Lord, when Your wonderful help came. I have no way to pay You, but at least I can tell You over and over, "thank You, thank You, thank You." And now, help us to get Your wonderful message of help to all of my people. Amen.'

"A long, respectful silence settled over those of us who waited with bowed heads. In some measure, each of us shared the former private torment and the present overwhelming relief of modern-day men from Gadarenes whom Jesus had touched with His Word."

18
You Are Not To Blame

D O YOU THINK I CAME TO BRING PEACE ON EARTH? NO, I
TELL YOU, BUT DIVISION—Jesus' words in LUKE 12:51/NIV.

KEN Jacobs sat nervously next to the Senator in the lawmaker's
mahogany-paneled library where shelves of books rose to meet the
room's lofty ceiling. Seated in a plush easy chair with a comfortable
back, Ken was decidedly uneasy. He had been summoned to the capitol city by SIL's Mexico director, John Daly, who was also in the room.
But all eyes were focused on Ken.

Senator Hugo B. Margaín Gleason had long supported SIL's presence in Mexico, but that presence had come under attack in the 1980s
from anthropologists and government officials who saw the U.S.-based
organization as a threat. "I'm having a hard time defending SIL," the
Senator advised. "I'm told you are teaching Indians not to salute the
Mexican flag, that you are telling Indian women they should be steril-
ized, and that you are dividing the tribe." He looked closely at Ken, who
had translated the NEW TESTAMENT for the Chamulas. "I know the others
aren't true, but is there any truth in that last charge about dividing the
tribe?" questioned the Senator.

Ken hesitated. What could he tell the Senator to explain the tribal expulsions which had escalated since the mid-1970s? Then Ken remembered a Chamula man, Mach, with whom he had spoken briefly one soggy afternoon a few years ago.

ᕯ ᕯ ᕯ ☿ ᕯ ᕯ ᕯ

ALL day long Mach labored strenuously to hoe a field perched precipitously on the mountainside. Ragged clothes hanging from his scrawny frame and sweat dripping from his brow, the man flailed relentlessly against weeds threatening to choke emerging corn plants. If this corn survived and produced an average crop, he could supply his wife, Xunca, with enough maize to feed them both and their tiny son, Miquel, until next harvest. With a bumper crop, he could sell a portion and buy a sheep to produce wool. Xunca could weave a thicker blanket to keep Miquel warm next winter. The baby was so small and always seemed cold.

As the sun sank toward the western horizon, Mach worked his way up the field, clearing weeds from one more row before shouldering the hoe and climbing the remaining distance to his family's home. Nearing the one-room house, he looked up, expecting to see a familiar plume of smoke wafting from the thatched roof. The smoke would serve as an outward sign of the activity inside. At this time of day, Xunca would be placing newly pressed tortillas on a clay griddle perched above the fire. Mach's pace quickened and his mouth began to water at the thought of food being prepared for his empty stomach. It had been a long time since his midday break, when he ate a few cold tortillas that Xunca had stuffed in his *nuti* before sunrise.

But he saw no smoke, and his heart sank. He knew immediately what had taken place. While laboring in the field, his father-in-law had come and taken Xunca and Miquel away. In part, Xunca's father was angry with Mach for violating tradition, and in part he feared the neighbors would retaliate against his daughter and his new little grandson—all because of Mach's transgressions. Mach had begun listening to the *Good New Words*.

Earlier while working in the Las Casas marketplace, Mach met a friend from a neighboring *paraje*. The friend described how his own son had been healed from a deadly illness when the evangelical believers prayed for him. The friend and his family had begun to believe in this healing God. As a result, they were expelled from their home in Chamula. The friend now lived in Las Casas, in a small outbuilding behind a large Spanish home, where his wife served as a maid. When he could, the man found work in the marketplace. But he seemed happy, and Mach was intrigued that his friend would give up so much to follow this new God. When his friend invited Mach to the Jacobs' yard to hear more, Mach decided to go. The appealing Words and the hope he saw in the believers' eyes kept him coming back. Unfortunately someone outside that infamous yard observed his comings and goings, and reported them to the tribe. Hearing the rumors, his father-in-law confronted Mach, insisting that he stop associating with the evangelicals. When his son-in-law refused, the older man threatened to take his daughter back.

Arriving home from the field that evening to the absence of smoke, Mach realized his father-in-law had made good on his threat. The house was deserted. His family was missing, along with his wife's few belongings. Mach's heart was as empty as his stomach. For one moment, Mach considered sharpening his machete and going to his father-in-law's house to settle his account and retrieve what was rightfully his. But that course of action did not square with the character of the God in whom he had begun to believe. Instead, Mach dropped his hoe and headed toward the old Spanish city, Las Casas.

The moon had replaced the sun in the darkened sky as Mach approached the city. Winding his way through the lamp-lit cobblestone streets, he arrived at the familiar walls surrounding the yard of Ken and Elaine Jacobs. Behind these walls he had listened so carefully as his countrymen read from the almost completed Chamula NEW TESTAMENT. Those words had spoken hope to this poor man's soul.

Mach rapped at the gate and Ken himself opened it to him. It had rained, as it does in the highlands most every afternoon from May to October, and the bare patch of dirt on which the two men stood was punctuated with puddles. Mach, who had never spoken personally with *Senior* Jacobs, looked down at the ground in respect while trying to frame his words. Some thoughts seemed to come easier as he worked the mud back and forth with his foot. Still peering down, he began to describe the loss he had suffered that very afternoon. As he finished his story, Mach collected his courage and asked the tall translator the question that had churned in his heart all the way down the mountain. "Canuto, how do I get my wife and baby back?"

Years later, sitting in the Senator's opulent library in Mexico City, Ken could still hear that question ringing in his ears. Now he knew how to answer the Senator's inquiry concerning whether SIL was dividing the tribe. Briefly, Ken told the official of Mach's visit to the Jacobs' home and of his burning question. "Senator," said Ken, "I told that Chamula man, 'It's the easiest thing in the world to get your family back—just return to the traditions of your tribe. Greet the sun god *Ch'ultotic* as you always did. Place your trust in the *j'ilols* and the *brujos*. Associate with the traditionalists in the *cabildo*, and drink the holy *pox* with your friends and relatives like you always did. In no time, your father-in-law will see you as you always were, and he'll return your wife and baby'."

The Senator still listened as Ken continued: "For a long time, Mach stood silently, churning the mud with his big toe. Finally, he spoke. 'Before I heard the *Good New Words*, I lived like an animal. The sun was my god, the witchdoctors were the hope of my body, and alcohol was the joy of my soul. Now, I am hearing that, through Jesus, I can be a son of God ... Canuto, I can't live the old way anymore'."

"To which, Senator, I quietly said, 'Well, Mach, *that* is your problem'."

Ken finished his story and looked again at Senator Margaín. At first his host was lost in thought. Then he abruptly concluded the meeting. "You're not to blame for dividing the Chamulas," the Senator announced to Ken and the others. "It's the message of that Book you are translating that is transforming the Chamulas."

Rising, the Senator escorted his guests through the front door, across a small patio, and out to the gate, beyond which the streets of Mexico City buzzed with activity. Before opening the gate, Senator Margaín bade his guests farewell with these parting words. "Let's always tell the truth of the work of SIL," he admonished them soberly. Then, pointing his index finger to the sky, he smiled and stated, "We'll have Him, up there, to defend us."

But less reasonable voices continued to exert pressure on SIL as their translators labored to finish their SIL contracts before leaving the country. When representatives of the Chamula Presbyterian churches at Colonia Betania, Getsemani, Nueva Esperanza, Palestinia, and Vista Hermosa approached Wycliffe Bible Translators to request the OLD TESTA-MENT be translated into the Chamula language, their request was politely declined.[103] At Wycliffe's suggestion, church leaders approached the Mexican Bible Society which agreed to sponsor the translation. The Society would pay half the translators' salaries if the Chamula Church was willing to pay the other half. An agreement was signed, and the effort to produce the entire Chamula Bible began in late 1988 with two indige-nous translators and with Ken Jacobs as coordinator of the project.

The churches chose Mariano Cashlan and Salvador Patishtán Díaz to translate the OLD TESTAMENT. This was remarkable since only twenty-five years before neither man could read or write the Chamula language. Now they worked at computers to transfer God's Word into the language of their people. The two men received schooling in the principles of translation and were charged with preparing a draft of each book of the OLD TESTAMENT. Once drafted, Ken worked with the translators to perfect each book, in con-sultation with OLD TESTAMENT scholar Bob Bascom from the Mexican Bible Society. Next, a revision committee of Chamula pastors and laymen would review each book, from GENESIS to MALACHI, to make sure it was understand-able. The coordinator, Ken, and a Chamula assistant would then read through each book and make final edits, with Bob spot-checking their work.

By now, Chamula believers were spreading the *Good New Words* wherever they went. They took the message to the coffee *fincas* on the Pacific Coast and to the Lacondon Jungle along the Mexican-Guatemalan border, where Chamulas had been moving since the 1960s to escape over-crowding in the highlands. It was there that Gustavo first heard the *Good New Words*—in music.

---

[103] The mission of Wycliffe/SIL is to translate at least the NEW TESTAMENT into every Bibleless language group of the world. Translation of the OLD TESTAMENT (or selected sections or books) is a branch-to-branch decision that depends upon assessment of cultural/tribal needs.

19
The Words in Music

G USTAVO GIRÓN RUÍZ was the Chamula man chosen by the cooperating churches to assist Ken Jacobs with the final edits to the OLD TESTAMENT. Gustavo's family home was *paraje* Ikal Lumtic, although he was born in San Juan Chamula because his father was in charge of a festival at the tribal center, and had taken his family to live there when his wife gave birth to Gustavo.

His father died soon afterward, and Gustavo's mother remarried. When Gustavo was five, his stepfather moved the family 130 miles south to a jungle farming community commonly known as Pacayal. To ease the population explosion in the highlands, the government had offered each family who relocated to the jungle forty acres of national forest land to develop. The settlers cleared and sold the two- to three-hundred-foot-tall mahogany trees from their land. Next they planted groves of coffee to sell as a cash crop, in addition to raising corn, beans, squash, and bananas.

Although the Chamulas who settled Pacayal imported their traditional beliefs, they were generally more open to new ideas than their highland relatives—perhaps because they now lived so far away from the tribal center. Dependent upon the government for basic services like roads and electricity and on the outside world for their livelihood,[104] many learned Spanish. In this environment, the Roman

---

[104] Chamulas in Pacayal and surrounding colonies had more interaction with the outside world because of their trade in hardwoods and coffee.

Catholic Church had greater success establishing chapels and training young men as catechists to propagate the faith, which was still a blend of animism and Christianity.[105]

The music of the Catholic Church at Pacayal attracted Gustavo. The priest oversaw churches in several villages, so he trained catechists to perform most non-sacramental duties including leading the worship music. A local catechist named Pedro took Gustavo, age twelve, under his wing. He encouraged Gustavo to practice both his guitar and singing. Later he included Gustavo in a musical group that traveled to area churches.

With his love of the music came an interest in the spiritual messages of the songs. Before his thirteenth birthday, Gustavo agreed to be trained as a catechist. For the first time this new role put him in contact with the Bible, in Spanish, which he eagerly read and began to view as the standard for life.

But that presented a problem. Gustavo observed that catechists were being selective in what they taught the people. For instance, they would not talk about the Scriptures that prohibited worship of other gods, which the Chamulas did in their festivals and by patronizing the shamans. Also, the manner in which the catechists lived their own lives did not square with what Gustavo was reading in God's Word. For one thing, they would sing in church on Sunday morning and then sing in the *cantinas* (saloons) at night. "While we're here," they rationalized, "we may as well have a glass or two." But it often didn't stop until they were drunk.

On several occasions Gustavo brought these apparent contradictions to the attention of his fellow catechists. "We're partly body and partly spirit," reasoned an older catechist, trying to help his young friend with conflicting feelings. "If we're in the churches praising God, that satisfies our spiritual side, and if we're singing in the bars where people are getting drunk, that satisfies our physical side."

That answer did not satisfy Gustavo. "It's like I've got two lords," he thought. "One Lord is served when I sing in church and the other is served when I sing in the bars." It bothered Gustavo that he was doing both. But he enjoyed music of all kinds, so he continued singing in the bars—and he passed his love of music along by teaching two other

---

[105] **Alan John Schreuder** (June 2001), *A History of the Rise of the Chamula Church*—Master's Thesis (Pasadena CA: Fuller Theological Seminary, School of World Mission and Institute of Church Growth), pg. 109.

young men from Pacayal how to play guitar. Javier Hernández Pérez and Andrés Ruíz Pérez also became catechists.

The three became fast friends, practicing their music, studying the Bible, and traveling the area as catechists. As they traveled, the trio discussed the contradictions in their lives. "Why is it that we believe in the Christianity of the Bible most of the year, but at certain times of the year we add on the traditions of our people," they wondered, referring to the drunken fiestas with Chamulas dancing around, imitating bulls and monkeys. They asked fellow catechists about this mixture of tradition and Christianity. Most shrugged it off.

"The people don't always like what we have to say, so we have to be careful to combine God's Word with the feelings and traditions of the people," another catechist tried to rationalize. "If we tell them they are sinners and that what they are doing is not right, they're going to get angry and not listen at all, so we have to tone it down a bit."

Finally, Gustavo, Javier, and Andrés worked up the courage to approach their priest about drinking and about mixing Christianity with other religious traditions.

"Don't worry about it," answered the priest, brushing off their question concerning animistic traditions. "Just leave it alone and go on being a catechist." On the issue of drinking he shrugged, "I have a glass or two of liquor myself and it's not a problem. If you don't want to get drunk, that's up to you, but don't be judging others and saying it's wrong, because it's not that big of a deal."

Gustavo and his friends were stunned. "On the one hand, we're being taught to follow the Bible and to do what the Bible says, and on the other hand we're being told, 'Go ahead and do these things. It's not a problem'." How could they continue to be wishy-washy about something so important? As it happened, the trio's choice of music decided the question.

In 1983, a tall merchant by the name of Lorenzo López Diáz from the colony of expulsed believers at Betania began traveling to the colonies in the Lacondon jungle. Among other things, Natil (tall) Lorenzo sold a light-weight fabric the women in Pacayal used to make skirts.[106] On Sundays he would visit the local Catholic Church, pull out

---

[106] The black wool skirts fabricated and worn by Chamula women in the highlands proved too heavy for the heat and humidity of the jungle.

his guitar, and begin playing and singing until he gathered a crowd; then he would show them a copy of the *Good New Words* in the Chamula language. Gustavo was fascinated by Lorenzo's music. The messages in songs like WHEN WE GO TO BE WITH JESUS and THE BIBLE TELLS US WE'LL RECEIVE A GIFT clearly matched the message of the Spanish Bible which had touched Gustavo's heart. As he learned these songs and conversed with Lorenzo about the *Good New Words*, Gustavo took seriously God's offer to lose his sin and manage his life.

Energized by this new Christian music, Gustavo and his companions began singing these songs in the Catholic church. Trouble soon followed. Other catechists and some in the congregations began to criticize the music. "You can't sing those Protestant songs in church," they complained.

"Why are these Protestant songs?" asked the trio, defending their choice of music. "Just because we haven't learned them before doesn't make them Protestant. They are songs from the Bible that praise God."

But their critics insisted, "You must sing Catholic songs!"

The conflict raged for several months. Once when Gustavo was leading the singing, a church official took hold of his guitar strap and dragged Gustavo and his guitar out of the church, yelling, "We're sick of that music; if that's the only music you have to sing we don't want to hear it any more."

Hurt, tired of the conflict, and confused at the anger generated by music which they believed honored God, Gustavo, Javier, and Andrés resigned as catechists. One Sunday Morning in August of 1987, Gustavo rose from his seat in the Catholic church at Pacayal and addressed the congregation.

"Brothers and Sisters," he began. "I've been your catechist and your teacher for a long time, but I disagree with what is going on. You say you believe God's Word, but the things you do and the things you say don't agree with God's Word, and it's as if you don't even care." The ex-catechist pointed to the festivals and the drunkenness of the leaders and the dispute over the music used in church as examples. "You can believe what you want, but I'm not going to stay with you any more," he concluded. "I'm not sneaking away. I'm telling you publically that I'm leaving."

Soon afterwards, Gustavo, Javier, and Andrés began meeting on Sunday mornings to sing their music in the house of Gustavo's parents.

Pacayal authorities immediately summoned the trio to appear before the town council. "You know there is an agreement in this town that no other religions will be permitted," said the town president. Although they had not affiliated with any other religious group to this point, they were being judged to be of a 'different' religion. Gustavo, Javier, and Andrés were threatened repeatedly with jail and expulsion if they did not return to the Catholic Church.

That very night the three young men hiked to a neighboring community to seek the counsel of *Senior* Castellano. This elder statesman had been involved in the original incorporation of the jungle colonies and had recently become a believer in the *Good New Words*. He and a local lawyer helped Gustavo, Javier, and Andrés appeal to the Federal government, which quickly sent a delegation to Pacayal. "These men have the freedom to practice whatever religion they choose," the delegation informed the local authorities.[107]

While the Federal government prevented their expulsion, the believers meeting in Gustavo's parents' house had to overcome many obstacles before they were accepted by the community. They affiliated with the Mexican Presbyterian Church and eventually constructed a church building in the community's center. With Javier Hernández Pérez as its pastor, this church grew to an adult membership of nearly three hundred persons, including sister congregations in three nearby towns and a mission outreach in a fourth. The two other ex-catechists, Andrés Ruíz Pérez and Gustavo Girón Ruíz, both played major roles in this growth, and in the 1990s they volunteered many hours to help translate the OLD TESTAMENT for their people into the language of their hearts.

"It was through music that the Gospel began to spread here," noted Gustavo, as he reflected on the path taken by the *Good New Words* in transforming his life and the lives of many Chamulas in the Lancondon jungle of southern Mexico.

---

[107] In asserting freedom of religion in the Lancondon jungle, the government had less to lose than it did in the highlands, where the party in power counted on tribal leaders to deliver the votes to keep it in power.

20
Now God Also Speaks Chamula

THE FIRST Chamula translation of the OLD TESTAMENT (in which Gustavo participated) and the third revision of the NEW TESTAMENT took fourteen years from the day the Chamula churches signed their contract with the Mexican Bible Sociey, to the day this entirely completed Bible rolled off the press. The churches took up a collection every Sunday morning, never once missing a payment to the translators.

Meanwhile the expulsions continued. But as quickly as the *caciques* drove small bands of believers out of the tribe, new believers took their place. Rather than dissuading them, ongoing persecution seemed to strengthen their faith and encourage them to share it with family and friends. As time passed, the Chamula traditionalists appeared to tire of expelling friends and family, with no apparent effect on the spread of Christianity. In the late 1980s and early 1990s, non-believing residents of some Chamula communities even refused the tribal authorities' orders to attack the Christians.[108]

Then came one of the most intense periods of persecution. Over the course of ten months, approximately eight hundred men, women, and children were expelled from eighteen villages. On September 8, 1993, many of those recently expelled believers began staging a sit-in in a courtyard at the Bureau of Indigenous Affairs in San Cristóbal de Las Casas. Within weeks, the number of peaceful protesters grew until a

108 **Alan John Schreuder** (June 2001), *A History of the Rise of the Chamula Church*—Master's Thesis (Pasadena CA: Fuller Theological Seminary, School of World Mission and Institute of Church Growth), pp. 118–122.

total of 584 refugees—without adequate food, medical attention, or sanitary conditions—occupied the compound. The believers' year-long sit-in gained international attention. Fortunately it ended with the return of all 584 Chamula believers to their home *parajes*. The resulting peace treaty marked the beginning of the end of the expulsions of believers from San Juan Chamula.[109]

However, one 'chance' meeting in that crowd of 584 displaced Chamulas revealed something of God's bigger purposes. Ken and Elaine Jacobs had briefly returned 'home' to San Cristóbal de Las Casas to meet with the OLD TESTAMENT revision committee, having been absent from San Cristóbal for thirteen years after completing their primary SIL assignment.[110] While there, the Jacobs took time to visit the believers camped in the government courtyard. The indigenous church had grown far beyond the small group which had its origins in the Jacobs' yard. Most of the men and women in the government courtyard were new believers and knew nothing of the Jacobs; likewise, Ken and Elaine knew none of them.

"All were living under the most miserable conditions," described Ken. "Some of the men still showed black and blue bruises from having been stoned by their fellow tribesmen."

As the Jacobs moved through the crowd, speaking words of encouragement to the refugees, one bright young man in his early thirties became curious about the Jacobs' ability to speak Chamula. *Chca'i ti ta xac'oponic ta jc'opcutique. C'usi xavutic?...* "I hear you speaking our language. How is this possible?" he asked.

Ken, now in his seventies, told the story of his friend Juan Pérez Jolote from *paraje* Cuchulumtic who, thirty-five years earlier, had patiently helped him take the first steps to learn the Chamula language. Then it was Ken's turn to be surprised, as the young man introduced himself. With a wide grin, he revealed, "Juan Pérez Jolote was my uncle!" Gesturing at the crowd, the young man added, "I, and many of these persecuted believers in this courtyard—we are from *paraje* Cuchulumtic."

[109] **Arthur Bonner** (1999), *We Will Not Be Stopped* (Universal Publisher/Upublish.com, pp. 111–117, 158).

[110] The Jacobs had not maintained a residence in the old Spanish City since 1980. Most of their work on the OLD TESTAMENT could now be done in other locations, with only brief trips back to Chiapas for occasional meetings.

Ken was gloriously stunned. Though Juan Pérez died as a non-believing Chamula traditionalist, the language assistance he'd given Ken ultimately resulted in delivery of the *Good New Words* to Juan's own people, and in the eternal salvation of Juan's very descendants. "What a thrilling reminder," wrote Ken later, in a letter to their prayer and financial supporters, "that the work of language learning and Bible translation is a most valid activity, and if we faint not, it brings great reward."

As the Chamula OLD TESTAMENT neared completion, the Jacobs received other confirmations concerning the extent to which God's Word had penetrated and expanded the community of believers. Evangelical leaders informed Ken that believers were now worshipping openly in nine different *parajes* throughout Chamula. "Their neighbors are hearing Christian hymns being sung in their familiar tongue and many of them are asking about the book they have heard is coming," reported the leaders. "By the time the whole Bible is published, hundreds of these neighbors will want to buy the Book."

Another eye-opening confirmation occurred one Sunday morning in 1997, when Ken and Elaine, on another return visit to Las Casas, 'happened' to walk past the door of *Caridad*, the second oldest Roman Catholic Church in the city. The Spanish conquerors had built this church with forced labor. Many of the hands that laid its centuries-old blocks belonged to Chamulas.

Now the grand old church overflowed with hundreds of Chamula Indians who spilled out of the large wooden doors into the street. The crowd on the outside stood on tiptoes trying to determine what was going on inside. "Could this be a healing ceremony?" thought Ken. Chamula shamans often bring their patients all the way into San Cristóbal to perform their healing ceremonies next to the colorful altars of a Mexican Catholic Church—such is the nature of syncretism.[111] "The patient must be an important Chamula to command such a large crowd of onlookers," thought Ken. Squeezing by the onlookers, Ken pushed his way through the crowded entrance. His height advantage rewarded him with a clear view over the shorter Maya crowd standing behind the last row of benches, all completely filled. What he saw was not what he

---

[111] **Syncretism** — a missiological term used to described the co-mingling of a traditional religion with Christianity. The mixture of animism and Catholicism is very common within the indigenous peoples of southern Mexico.

expected. Turning back toward the door, he beckoned to Elaine. "You have to come in and see and hear this," he whispered, excitedly.

In that old colonial church, the Jacobs witnessed far more than a mere physical healing ceremony. They watched as the Word of God washed and cleansed the minds and hearts of a people stained by sin. The Word was not spoken in Spanish, which the Chamulas did not really understand, but in their own unique Tzotzil dialect. The speaker read from the same Chamula NEW TESTAMENT which Ken and Elaine had spent years translating. The speaker's message originated from the book of HEBREWS. "Jesus took His own blood and went into the very presence of the Holy of Holies," said the speaker. "My Brethren, just think, because of Jesus we are free from our sins. Now we know we are accepted by God."

The following Sunday, the Jacobs returned to *Caridad Church*, anxious to meet and commend these Chamula Catholic leaders for their love and respect for the Word of God. Ken observed, "We have never met you, but you obviously hold the *Good New Words* in high regard and take great joy in sharing them with hundreds of your friends and neighbors who are spiritually hungry." Ken then described the progress that was being made on the OLD TESTAMENT.

"We have heard the whole Bible is being translated into our language, and we eagerly anticipate its arrival," replied the Catholic leaders. Ken had the pleasure of confirming that the whole Bible would soon be available in their own heart language.

ᕁ ᕁ ᕁ 𝄞 ᕁ ᕁ ᕁ

On November, 25, 2001, the day finally arrived. The Chamula churches hosting the celebration rented 7,500 chairs and set them up in a soccer field-sized lot with a stage at one end. The stage was elevated to give those attending a good view of speakers, which included the Roman Catholic Bishop of the San Cristóbal diocese, the Mayor of San Cristóbal, the head of the federal government's Internal and Religious Affairs, and representatives from the Mexican Bible Society. The Governor of Chiapas also sent his representative, along with a contribution of 40,000 pesos to purchase soda pop and sweet bread for the crowd gathered to dedicate the completed Chamula Bible. A sign draped across the platform that late autumn day declared: *Dios Habla También A Chamula...* "Now God Also Speaks Chamula."

On one side of this large field, each Chamula church set up individual booths to sell copies of the Chamula Bibles when the ceremonies ended. The churches had asked for 20,000 copies, but only 10,000 had been delivered. The Mexican Bible Society assured them the remaining 10,000 would be printed and delivered as soon as the first copies were sold. The Bishop of Chiapas, Monsignor Felipe Arizmendi Esquivel, promised the Chamula community he would secure funding for the remaining 10,000.

A bedazzling *azul* canopy crowned the valley of grass that crisp, sunlit morning. People in cars, taxis, or on foot streamed out of Las Casas toward the celebration in Nueva Esperanza. By 10:00 A.M. the chairs were filled with Chamulas, plus hundreds more crowding the aisles and spaces between occupied chairs. A large gathering of young people, many of whom were born after their parents were forced from their homes, watched from the high flat cement roof of a nearby government school. Eyewitnesses estimated the crowd at 10,000. About 200 were Ladino and American. The rest were Chamula believers and their guests, including friends and family from the tribe. Would some of these guests be the next to embrace the *Good New Words*?

As the ceremony began, Abner López, Director of the Mexican Bible Society, presented copies of the Chamula Bible to Mariano Cashlan, Salvador Patishtán Díaz, Gustavo Girón Ruíz, Andrés Ruíz Pérez, and others involved in the translation effort. Then, one by one, the dignitaries addressed the people. All spoke in Spanish while a Chamula leader interpreted their words to the indigenous assembly.

Finally, Ken and Elaine stood before the crowd. Only a small percentage of the large throng assembled knew this couple with wavy white hair. But as Ken began to speak, a hush fell over the sea of Chamula faces in front of him. Though he was a *cashlan* in appearance, everyone recognized how skillfully this man employed the language of their hearts. The translator, now eighty years of age and having recently retired from active service, read from LUKE Chapter Three of the new Chamula Bible. In this passage, a man named Simeon, whom God had promised would not die until he laid eyes on the Christ, took the child Jesus in his arms and prayed to God. Ken could identify with Simeon. He, too, had seen God's promise fulfilled as his life's work, the Chamula Bible, was about to be distributed to thousands. Ken read Simeon's prayer that stunning November day and made it his own. "Sovereign Lord," he began, "as You have promised, You may now dismiss Your servant in peace. For my eyes have seen Your salvation, which You have prepared in the sight of all people...".

As Ken spoke, Elaine surveyed the vast expanse of souls covering the grassy field in front of the stage. The Word of God had now come to them in full measure. She wept quietly as she thought, "It was worth it all!"

21
Blessed Beyond Belief

K EN AND ELAINE JACOBS returned yet again to San Cristóbal de Las Casas in 2006 to see with their own eyes the effect God's Word has had on the Chamula nation. What they now saw amazed them. They counted fourteen thriving Chamula communities surrounding the old Spanish city and extending south along the Pan American highway—many with Biblical names like Bethany, Galilee, and Palestine. None existed in the 1950s when the Jacobs arrived in southern Mexico, and the first of these new towns had just begun to develop when they sold their Las Casas property in 1980 and moved northward to the Mexican state of Hidalgo.

Twenty-six years later the Jacobs drove along the *Periferico*, the ring road encircling Las Casas. They could hardly believe what they were seeing. This road did not exist when they lived in Las Casas, and their most common recollection of those early years was watching raggedly dressed Chamula Indians leading burros loaded with charcoal down the city's narrow cobblestone streets. Now this big thoroughfare was loaded with cars, taxis, prospering businesses, churches, and Chamula Christians by the thousands living in the hills along the *Periferico*. "We were just overwhelmed," exclaimed Ken "by the positive changes we observed in the lives and fortunes of those who had been expelled from tribal lands for following the *Good New Words*. We could hardly take in what we were seeing."

Economic Transformation

To those who gave up everything to follow Him, God seems to have extended a special blessing. Such is the case for Paxcu López Hernández, whose house burned to the ground in the 1967 fire, shotgun, and machete attack that injured Paxcu and her niece Abelina, and killed the other three children in her charge. Today Paxcu, her husband, and their four children own and operate a family store and restaurant along the Pan American highway in Betania. Paxcu reported to Ken and Elaine that her story is common among believers. "Not only do I feel God's mercy in my life, but I am seeing that He is being merciful to Chamulas all around me," she observed. "Many of my people left with nothing but folded hands. Everything was lost. But they've really gained. God loves us and takes care of our needs." Everywhere they went, Ken and Elaine met Chamulas with similar stories:

Thirty-five-year-old Domingo López owns and operates a taco shop along the *Periferico*. Domingo's family fled *paraje* Nich´en when he was seven. With three years' education, the young man worked as a mason's helper and a stevedore until 1988 when he started his own restaurant. Today that restaurant, which he operates alone, provides a living for his wife and their six children.

Domingo Hernández Gómez owns a hardware store in Colonia Hormiga. As a young man, he planted corn, picked coffee, drove a mini-bus—and little by little saved enough money to purchase a tortilla-making machine before starting his hardware store in 1990. Today his children run the hardware store and the tortilla manufacturing business next door, while Domingo serves as an elder in his church and sings in a musical group ministering to house churches in Chamula. "The good Lord was my teacher and without a doubt I am the beneficiary of his care," declared Domingo.

Manuel Díaz owns an audio tape and compact disk business that ships 50,000 labels annually. His father died from drinking before Manuel was born. His mother fed four children by chopping wood and gathering moss for sale as sponges. She believed the *Good New Words* and was driven out of *paraje* Sactzu when Manuel was seven. Manuel Diaz loves to sing, and now in his mid-thirties he helps indigenous musicians distribute their work throughout Mexico and Guatemala. "There was nothing for us in Chamula," claimed Manuel of the change. "Now we have eternal life, and we are better off financially."

Expulsed Chamula believers did not achieve economic success overnight, and some still struggle financially. When they left the tribe, most were subsistence farmers and could find jobs only as manual laborers. Chamula women swept the city streets of Las Casas and Chamula men unloaded trucks in the marketplace. Over the years, their skill levels and standard of living has improved markedly.

Al Schreuder[112] has worked as teacher and mentor with the Chamula Church for as long as Ken and Elaine have been gone from Las Casas. "The economic development of the Chamula believers has just been incredible," Al reported to Ken. "They once worked *for* the merchants who owned stalls in the marketplace, but now the Chamulas *own* the stalls." Al cites José Hernández Gómez, the son of a Chamula expelled from the *paraje* Chic´bilte´nal in 1979, as an example: "José is now the preferred retailer for all fruits and vegetables for the nearby Mexican military base." Al also notes that Chamulas now own many of the 2,000 taxis and mini-buses which operate as the public transportation system in the narrow streets of Las Casas.

One of those taxi owners, Pedro González, learned of the *Good New Words* from his father-in-law in 1983. "I heard the Word well, and it was about four months after I first believed that we were driven out of *paraje* Colinda," he confirmed with Ken. "Traditionalists where I lived burned a lot of Scripture, and we were told to give up what we believed. Many of us were put into prison, and I decided it was better

[112] Al and Sue Schreuder are missionaries of the Reformed Church of America, working with Chamulas under the auspices of the Mexican Presbyterian Church.

to leave than to give up the Word of God." After twelve years of sewing clothes to support his family, Pedro bought an old car and began hauling merchandise and other freight between Chamula and San Cristóbal. Little by little his business grew. Today, he owns two taxis with hired drivers, as well as a comfortable house for his wife and five children. He attributes his success to hearing God's Word. "If I had never heard the *Good New Words*, I would probably be an alcoholic and beating my wife," says the now-successful business owner.

Social Transformation

In addition to economic advancement, the Word of God also created positive social gains for Chamula believers. Because of the violent nature of their expulsion, Chamulas were the first indigenous group permitted to live in, and around, Las Casas. Together with other indigenous groups who migrated to the old Spanish City, these first and second generation immigrants now comprise nearly half the city's population. The infusion of their culture has greatly enhanced the economy, by attracting increased tourism.[113] Though prejudice still exists, Chamulas found greater acceptance within the larger Mexican community, and the Bible's message has changed the believers' hearts toward Ladinos.

"From the beginning, the Mestizo[114] community has been very racist and has always exploited the indigenous communities," said Abdías Tovilla Jaime, Ladino pastor, lawyer, and president of The Good Samaritan Human Rights Organization. "Since arriving in the city, there are about 15,000 Indians who basically control the transportation service and the market. The Mestizos have learned to accept that. The Chamulas, in their hearts, have always hated Mestizos. But since they've heard the Word of God, they've learned to forgive. Pedro González agrees. "There was a time when we first began to stream into Las Casas that the community said, 'Go back where you came from.' But that seems to have dissipated. We're so much a part of the community now that they no longer tell us to leave."

---

[113] **Jan Rus** (2007), *The New Mayan City in the Valley of Jovel: Rapid Urbanization, Indigenous Youth, and Community in San Cristóbal de las Casas* (Riverside CA: Latin American Studies), pp. 8–12; *cf.* Footnote #98.

[114] **Mestizo** — similar to *Ladino*.

Education Transformation

The Chamulas have also gained educationally. Expulsed Chamula believer Manuel Vacos went back to school after working ten years as a bricklayer. He received his certification to teach and most recently taught two first-grade classes at a bilingual public school in Nueva Esperanza. He showed Ken first, second, third, and fourth grade textbooks in the written language of Chamula that the Jacobs introduced only a few decades earlier. "Our expulsion has turned into a blessing," Vacos emphasized. "The young people here get a better education. As a result, their economic situation improves. Those who still live back in Chamula, what do they get? Some of them aren't even educated."

Chamula children in the Christian *colonias* transition to Spanish-only lessons in third and fourth grades, and their Chamula written language provides the helpful bridge to do so. Al Schreuder told Ken, "Over a period of time, the Chamula believers have seen the value of education and of learning Spanish to help them better integrate into the Mestizo world, at least in part. If you are going to be buying and selling in the market, you are buying and selling with people who speak Spanish."

Political Transformation

In recent years the expulsed Chamulas and their children have also begun making their voice heard in the political arena. Most Chamulas in government serve in lower level, appointed offices, but that is beginning to change. Political parties have begun looking for indigenous candidates for municipal and state positions. Most importantly, Chamula evangelicals are learning to express themselves at the ballot box. Abdias Tovilla says eighty to eighty-five percent of the believers are getting their credentials to register and vote properly. "This is something they have taken on as a way to make their voices heard and influence their government," he remarked. Pedro González told Ken that he views political participation as a natural part of living the Christian life. "We see from the book of ROMANS that we are to respect and honor the authorities. There are some who don't vote, but the believing Chamulas are beginning to participate in the voting process."

Spiritual Transformation

Despite amazing advancements in almost every area of their lives, Chamula believers have not forgotten their primary gain is spiritual. Thousands meet weekly to worship and hear the Word of God. "Probably the biggest thing we noticed is all the churches they've erected," observed Elaine, as she drove around the area. "Someone said there were almost one hundred evangelical churches the Chamulas have built on their own, with no money from the outside." By some estimates there are upwards of 30,000 believers, with that number still on the increase.

Blessed beyond belief, the Chamula Christians are reaching back into tribal highlands to friends and neighbors who have not yet trusted in the Lord Jesus Christ. Every Sunday, eighteen elders and twenty deacons of *Iglesia Betania* (Bethany Church) scatter to various communities in the Chamula highlands to share the Scripture. Pastor Domingo Hernández Hernández, himself jailed many times in the early years for his faith in Jesus Christ, reports men and women are eager to hear the *Good New Words*. "Our job is not just here in this church," he insists. "We continue to extend the Word of God, and we are even making movies that will go out to our companions in Chamula." He adds, "Wherever we go and give the Word of God, there are those who listen and believe." Today there is at least one house church in every one of the 124 *parajes* within Chamula's 1,000 square miles, and many villages have several congregations.

The elders of *Iglesia La Puerta del Cielo* (Doorway to Heaven Church) at Colonia Getsemani meet each week to assign duties for the next Sunday, including going out to lead worship at nine house churches in the Chamula highlands. Although major expulsions ceased after 1995, openly declaring one's Christianity can still be risky in some locations.

Pastor Chuz Hernández Hernández was jailed in 2002 as he served communion at a small house church near the tribal headquarters. "I went out to have communion with a little group that was just beginning," recalls the pastor. "I was just in the process of putting out the bread and wine, when the authorities came and arrested all sixteen of us. In jail, we began to sing, and it produced fear in the community."

After threatening the prisoners with violence if they continued to meet, the president of Chamula ordered their release. To avoid aggravating the authorities, Pastor Chuz suspended visits to the house church temporarily. Two months later the believers resumed bi-weekly services at the house church and have not been bothered since. However, tensions and threats of jailing, beatings, and other violence are still very real in many Chamula *parajes*.

Stories abound of individual Chamulas who give their time and resources to share the love of God with those who have not heard. After being jailed and evicted from their land in *paraje* Chiotic, Tumin Ch'ic and his family suffered an even greater loss for their faith in Jesus Christ. Tumin's uncle had returned to the village to retrieve some property. He was falsely accused of having burned a sacred cross belonging to the community, and murdered as a result. Two years later, after spending all their money on shamans, one of the men who conspired to kill Tumin's uncle brought his ailing father to Tumin's house in Las Casas.

Tumin and his family took care of the father and son in their home for nearly three years, buying their clothes, food, and medicine. While they cared for the men, they shared with them the *Good New Words*. Eventually the father died—but as a believer. After confessing to Tumin that he had burned the cross and blamed it on Tumin's uncle, the son also placed his faith in Christ, as have many people in Tumin's old village. "Little by little there were others who saw that we were good," insists Tumin. "We loved them. We treated them well. There are many today that are in the Kingdom because we took care of them."

The Gospel *is* penetrating the most spiritually dark regions of the 30-mile by 30-mile Chamula homeland. Natil Lorenzo, the tall lay evangelist from Betania who taught *Good New Words* songs to Gustavo Girón Ruíz, has repeatedly visited Tsonta Vits, the heart of witchcraft in Chamula. After a long journey by car, Lorenzo walks for two hours to reach this remote *paraje* where he makes friends by singing hymns translated into Chamula. "For eight Sundays I visited Tsonta Vits and now there is one man who has the desire to believe the Gospel!" Lorenzo excitedly told Ken. Because of this passion for evangelism, as exemplified by Natil Lorenzo, some Chamula Christians believe that one day the evangelicals will become the majority population in the tribe.

Outside Chamula, in the colonies formed by the expulsed Christians, another challenge presents itself—that of passing the *Good New Words* to the children and grandchildren of the first believers. Many of these young Chamulas know little of the persecution endured by their parents and grandparents. Leonardo de Jesús Méndez Méndez, the president of a Christian Indian youth association, placed his trust in Jesus when friends invited him to church. "I want to reach out to other young people who have not heard the Word of God and even those who may have heard but have not accepted it," declared Leonardo. "I want to help them in their leadership roles—to know how to pray, how to sing, and how to share the Word of God—so they, in turn, can be like the young people who brought me to the Lord."

WHAT effect did the Word of God have on the Chamula nation? Despite persecution, loss of property, the threat of death, and death itself, almost every aspect of the Chamula believers' lives markedly changed for the better: spiritually, economically, educationally, socially, and politically. Most importantly, Chamulas are reaching back to win their family and friends—to bless others with the blessing which God has given them through the Gospel of Jesus Christ. The importance of translating the Gospel into the Chamula dialect is underscored by the passionate words of Paxcu: "Emphatically, I declare that our ears are closed when we hear it in Spanish, but when we hear the Word of God in our language, it is as though our ears and eyes are opened. *C'anbeic ti Diose, ta xac'boxuc. Sa'ic, ta xataic. Tijic ti ti'nae, ta xajambatic* (Ask and it will be given to you; seek and you will find; knock and the door will be opened to you).[115] How well I hear God saying that to me in Chamula," Paxcu told her longtime friends, Ken and Elaine.

The Jacobs will be the first to tell you their roles in this amazing story were simply as messengers, sent to deliver the *Good New Words* in a way that would touch the hearts of Chamulas who would hear it

[115] MATTHEW 7:7/NIV.

well and believe. The Jacobs often quote a modern-day proverb learned late in life: "Efficiency is doing things right, but effectiveness is doing the right thing." They readily admit they were not always the most efficient, but God's Word has been proven ultimately effective, beyond their greatest expectations, as it indelibly changed the hearts and lives of these people—both now, and for eternity.

After witnessing these changes with his own eyes, Ken wishes others could travel to Chiapas to behold the amazing transformation the *Good New Words* have made in the lives of the Impossible People. "You will see," declares the eighty-five-year-old translator, his voice trembling with emotion. "You will marvel when you drive around this part of the world and talk to thousands of Chamulas; they're walking into the Kingdom of God because of what was right—the Word of God in their mother tongue."

This Amazing Story
A Translator's Postscript

THIS AMAZING STORY, still unfolding, didn't happen because Elaine and I were skillful strategists, well qualified to accomplish that about which you have been reading. Quite the contrary, we are two rather ordinary folks whom God used along with a supporting cast. He orchestrated our lives and circumstances to result in something of eternal significance.

Some have said that the Chamula story is our success story. That really is not true. The Chamula story was our school where Elaine and I learned that to succeed, we—like children—needed to do the right thing and to accept all the help we were offered.

God Chose Us

We are often asked why we chose to be Bible translators and why we chose to go to the Chamula Indians. We did neither. It was God's doing, not ours. It must have been God's interest in the Chamulas and His choice that we should have a role in His plans for them.

I grew up in a hard working Dutch farm family. In my grade school years, I prayed with my mother to accept Jesus as my Savior. But missionary work, much less Bible translation, never entered my mind as an activity I would consider for my life's work. But here's what happened to alter my thinking. God confirmed His protection on my life just before my battalion stormed Omaha Beach on D-Day, and gave me a desire to make my life count. This trumped my earlier plans to become an accountant and led me to St. Paul Bible College in St. Paul, Minnesota.

Elaine grew up in a Christian home and married a wonderful man who was killed in World War II when his bomber went down; this happened shortly before she birthed their first child, Joyce. Despite her grief, Elaine responded to God's call and enrolled at St. Paul Bible College where we met and married. Late in our studies, we decided to attend SIL (Summer Institute of Linguistics) training at the University of Oklahoma to prepare for missions work. Cameron Townsend, founder of Wycliffe, encouraged Elaine and me to consider becoming Bible translators. We said yes and Wycliffe eventually assigned us to the Chamula Indians of Southern Mexico. The rest is history.

God Orchestrated Our Lives and Circumstances

We needed to learn the Chamula language and reduce it to written form in order to translate the Scriptures, but the Chamulas would kill any outsider attempting to live among them. The situation seemed impossible, but not to God. He orchestrated our lives and circumstances by giving us a place to meet Chamulas outside and away from their tribe.

Soon after our assignment to the Chamulas, we adopted the newborn baby of an unwed mother who died during childbirth. The child's Spanish grandmother was the only living relative who had any interest in his well-being, and she was homeless. We went looking for a small property that 'Grandma' could call her own and ended up purchasing a two and one-half acre walled-in yard at an amazingly low price. Grandma passed away soon afterwards, but Elaine and I—and our newly-adopted son Jerry—moved to that property.

God's hand in giving us this property soon became evident as we hired Chamula men to work the garden and Elaine's medical ministry attracted ailing Chamulas—all behind the safety of those protective walls. This large yard became our language learning center. In time, it also served as a Bible translation center and a refuge for the first Chamula Christians.

God Gave Us a Supporting Cast

The Chamula Indians have the Scriptures, the Word of God, translated into their heart language. It didn't happen because of us alone. In addition to orchestrating our lives and circumstances, God also gave us a supporting cast, without which we would not have succeeded. There were those who took care of us—who bought our beans and tortillas, as the Chamulas would say. Individuals and congregations across the United States saw themselves as **Investors** in our God-given work. There were **Our Colleagues** who were like family to us and who (like Bob Longacre in Chapter 6) helped us succeed in analyzing the grammar, which led to good translation. Then, there were the **Intercessors**—those who prayed for the Chamulas and who prayed for us.

The first intercession began ten years before Elaine and I were asked to try to reach the Chamula Indians. In the late 1940s, Ken and Nadine Weathers were translating for a neighboring tribe, and they wondered how the difficult Chamulas could ever be reached. Nadine got a map from the Indian agency in Las Casas, listing names and locations of every single Chamula *paraje* (village or community). She cut the map into pieces, with each piece showing at least one *paraje* and sent the pieces to praying people all over the United States and Canada. Thirty years later, Elaine sat down with Domingo Hernández Aguilar, the first Chamula Christian, and they moved their fingers across a similar map. In every *paraje* they were able to identify Chamulas who had believed in the *Good New Words*.

Conclusion

We have finished that which was our original responsibility, the NEW TESTAMENT in the language of the Chamulas, and we were honored to be chosen to give the Chamulas the OLD TESTAMENT as well. Despite our limitations, God accomplished all this by orchestrating our circumstances, and by giving us a supporting cast.

What can we say? It is not hard to succeed when nobody will let you fail, not even God Himself.

J Kenneth Jacobs

KEN JACOBS
Spring 2009

Glossary

Selected Spanish, Chamula Tzotzil, and English Terms Used in this Book

Brujo *(broo•hoe)*

Harming shaman. *Brujo* is literally 'a giver of sickness and death.' For a fee, a *Brujo* readily places a curse on a person. *(Spanish)*

Cabildo *(kah•bil•doe)*

Town hall. *(Spanish)*

Cacique *(kah•see•kay)*

Tribal boss. *(Tzotzil* and *Spanish)*

Casblan *(cahsh•lahn)*

Outsiders, not of Maya Indian blood. *(Tzotzil)*

Ch'ulel *(chew•lel)*

A Maya Indian's soul. *(Tzotzil)*

Chamarro *(cha•mar•roe)*

A sleeveless woolen tunic, knee-length, fastened at the waist with a leather belt. *(Spanish)*

Chamula *(cha•mu•la)*

The term *Chamula* is used for one of four differing meanings:

■ **PEOPLE GROUP:** *Chamula* is the name of the indigenous Maya Indian tribe (people group) written about in this story. The current population of this people group is estimated at 150,000.

■ **LANGUAGE:** *Chamula* is the term used to identify this same people group's language dialect. Formally known as Chamula Tzotzil, it is one of at least two dozen Tzotzil dialects and sub-dialects. (Tzotzil is one of five Mayan language groups in Chiapas.)

■ **MUNICIPALITY (TOWN):** *Chamula* is the shortened name of the tribe's governmental and ceremonial center, San Juan Chamula.

■ **MUNICIPALITY (TRIBAL REGION):** *Chamula* is the name of the 30 mile by 30 mile municipal tribal region, located in the oak and pine forested highlands of Chiapas.

Chanul *(chah•nool)*

A companion animal soul given at birth. Chamulas believe they share their soul (*ch'ulel*) with an animal born at the same time. Illness or death is interpreted as distress or death of that person's animal—their *chanul*. *(Tzotzil)*

Chiapas *(chee•ah•pas)*

The southernmost state in Mexico, located on the southeast coast. Chiapas borders Guatemala on the east, and the Pacific Ocean on the south. Chiapas has an area of 28,653 square miles and a 2005 population of 4,293,459 people.

Finca *(fin•ca)*

Plantation. *(Spanish)*

Indian

A non-discriminatory term for indigenous Maya-descended residents, including Chamulas, in southern Mexico.

J'ilol *(ee•lol)*

Healing shaman. *J'ilol* is literally 'a sayer of words.' An *j'ilol* explains why someone is dying, then prescribes a cure. *(Tzotzil)*

Jacobs, Ken & Elaine

The Bible translators assigned in the late 1950s to the Chamula people, to learn their language and create its written alphabet. Throughout their 46 years of missionary work, the Jacobs lived in various locations in Mexico, including

Mitzitón and San Cristóbal de Las Casas in the southern-most state of Chiapas, and also at Wycliffe Bible Translators' linguistic center in the centrally-located state of Hidalgo. Chamulas often addressed Ken and Elaine in the Spanish equivalents of their names, *Canuto* and *Elena.*

Ladino *(lad•dee•no)* A Spanish-speaking Central American resident who is not of Indian descent. *(Spanish)*

Mayol *(my•yol)* Chamula tribal policeman. *(Tzotzil)*

Mitzitón *(mee•tsee•tone)* *Mitzitón* is a small 'breakaway' settlement of Chamula people located roughly nine miles south of San Cristóbal de Las Casas on the Pan American Highway. Bible translators Ken and Elaine Jacobs rented a ranch house here on a part-time basis between 1957 and 1964.

Moletique *(mol•e•teek•ey)* A council of wise people who perpetrate tradition and act as judges in deciding the most serious matters facing tribal leadership. *(Tzotzil)*

Nuti *(new•tee)* A bag slung from the shoulder used for carrying personal items. *(Tzotzil)*

Paraje *(pah•rah•hay)* Village or hamlet. *(Tzotzil and Spanish)*

Pox *(pōsh)* Sugar cane liquor. Chamulas consider *pox* to be the 'gift of the gods.' It is used heavily in all religious and civil ceremonies, and to announce an important conversation between individual Chamulas. *(Tzotzil)*

San Cristóbal de Las Casas The large colonial municipality and market town located in the Valley of Jobel, about six miles from San Juan Chamula. A Ladino-inhabited city back then, Bible translators Ken and Elaine Jacobs rented an apartment here from 1953 to 1962, then a small home from 1960 to 1961, and in 1962 they purchased a larger home in the city (a walled compound with a two-and-one-half-acre yard), where they lived and worked until 1979. *San Cristóbal de Las Casas* is often referred to by either of its shortened names, *San Cristóbal,* or simply *Las Casas.*

San Juan Chamula *San Juan Chamula* is the governmental and ceremonial center for the Chamula people, located on the central highlands of Chiapas about six miles north of San Cristóbal de Las Casas. The inhabitants of this oak and pine forested community are exclusively Chamulas.

Shaman *(shay•muhn)* Simplistically, a witchdoctor. In the traditional Chamula worldview, *shamans* are indispensable 'intermediaries' between the natural world and spiritual world. *Shamans* have a dual-purpose role, both to **heal** and to **harm**. Specific Chamula terms for *shamans* are:

■ *J'ILOL:* **Healing** shaman
■ *BRUJO:* **Harming** shaman.

Traditionalist A Chamula person who keeps and zealously enforces the cultural and religious traditions of the tribe.

Mexico Map

Selected Geographical Locations Referred to in This Book

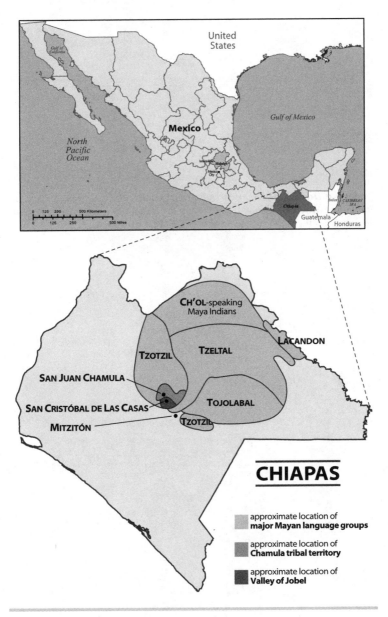

United States

Gulf of California

North Pacific Ocean

Mexico

Gulf of Mexico

Hidalgo

Mexico City

Chiapas

Guatemala

Honduras

CARIBBEAN SEA

0 125 250 500 Kilometers
0 125 250 500 Miles

CH'OL-speaking Maya Indians

LACANDON

TZOTZIL

TZELTAL

SAN JUAN CHAMULA

SAN CRISTÓBAL DE LAS CASAS

TZOTZIL

TOJOLABAL

MITZITÓN

CHIAPAS

approximate location of **major Mayan language groups**

approximate location of **Chamula tribal territory**

approximate location of **Valley of Jobel**